FROM FOUNDER TO FUTURE

GARLAND MILL
DESIGN + BUILD

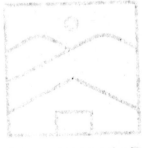

FROM FOUNDER
—— TO ——
FUTURE

A Business Road Map
to Impact, Longevity,
and Employee Ownership

JOHN ABRAMS

BK

Berrett–Koehler Publishers, Inc

Berrett-Koehler Publishers, Inc.
1333 Broadway, Suite P100
Oakland, CA 94612-1921
Tel: (510) 817-2277
Fax: (510) 817-2278
bkconnection.com

ORDERING INFORMATION

Quantity sales. Special discounts are available on quantity purchases by corporations, associations, and others. For details, please go to bkconnection.com to see our bulk discounts or contact bookorders@bkpub.com for more information.

Individual sales. Berrett-Koehler publications are available through most bookstores. They can also be ordered directly from Berrett-Koehler: Tel: (800) 929-2929; Fax: (802) 864-7626; bkconnection.com.

Orders for college textbook / course adoption use. Please contact Berrett-Koehler: Tel: (800) 929-2929; Fax: (802) 864-7626.

Distributed to the US trade and internationally by Penguin Random House Publisher Services.

The authorized representative in the EU for product safety and compliance is EU Compliance Partner, Pärnu mnt. 139b-14, 11317 Tallinn, Estonia, www.eucompliancepartner.com, +372 5368 65 02.

Berrett-Koehler and the BK logo are registered trademarks of Berrett-Koehler Publishers, Inc.

Printed in The United States of America.

Berrett-Koehler books are printed on long-lasting acid-free paper. When it is available, we choose paper that has been manufactured by environmentally responsible processes. These may include using trees grown in sustainable forests, incorporating recycled paper, minimizing chlorine in bleaching, or recycling the energy produced at the paper mill.

Library of Congress Cataloging-in-Publication Data

Names: Abrams, John, author.
Title: From founder to future : a business road map to impact, longevity, and employee ownership / John Abrams.
Description: Oakland, CA : Berrett-Koehler Publishers, Inc., [2025] | Includes bibliographical references and index.
Identifiers: LCCN 2024050608 (print) | LCCN 2024050609 (ebook) | ISBN 9781523006816 (paperback) | ISBN 9781523006823 (pdf) | ISBN 9781523006830 (epub)
Subjects: LCSH: Employee ownership. | Leadership.
Classification: LCC HD5650 .A27 2025 (print) | LCC HD5650 (ebook) | DDC 338.6/9—dc23/eng/20250204
LC record available at https://lccn.loc.gov/2024050608
LC ebook record available at https://lccn.loc.gov/2024050609

First Edition

33 32 31 30 29 28 27 26 25   10 9 8 7 6 5 4 3 2 1

Book production: Westchester Publishing Services UK
Cover design: Ashley Ingram and John Magnifico
Cover photograph: Alison Shaw

Dedicated to Kim Angell, my late-in-life partner and soulmate,
and to my kids and hers.

CONTENTS

——————— **PART THREE** Implementing the Five Transitions

FOREWORD

A Loving Look into the Future of Business

Ari Weinzweig
*Cofounding partner of Zingerman's
Community of Businesses*

I sure wish I'd had a copy of this book by John Abrams back in 1982, when my business partner Paul Saginaw and I opened Zingerman's Delicatessen. Yes, it's true that over the last forty-two years, we have managed to stumble and bumble our way into learning and practicing much of what John has shared in these pages. But our lives sure would have been a whole lot easier if we had been able to learn from John's words of wisdom.

If we had *From Founder to Future* back then, it would have allowed us to practice one of John's primary messages: Begin your business with the end in mind. Not in some doomscrolling, social-media-fed-fear-of-going-out-of-business way, but in the uplifting spirit of creating employee-owned, community-minded institutions that spread wealth and well-being as widely as possible. Instead of planning for Wall Street IPOs to generate more wealth for the founders, these businesses help to keep communities going for generations.

Over the last fifty years, John Abrams and his colleagues at South Mountain Company have demonstrated that cooperative models can be magical ways to do business. When employees are empowered to be active owners in the business of which they're a part, both they *and* the business do better. Dignity and doing the right thing are very much aligned with running a good business. No matter where your business is in its life cycle—starting up, middle age, or starting to think about succession—*From Founder to Future* is guaranteed to help guide you to a good place. The models that John describes in such helpful detail are, I believe, the future of business.

I first met John in the spring of 2012. I had read his 2008 book *Companies We Keep* as part of our own early explorations into what succession and more widely shared ownership might look like at Zingerman's. We were in the first few months of our thirtieth year in business and were finally beginning to grapple with how to handle succession. I found a couple of people who knew John. Introductory emails were sent, phone calls were made, conversations commenced, and a friendship began.

A year later, John flew out to Portland to share with us his learnings about employee ownership and succession planning at our annual partner meeting. What you have in your hands here is essentially the wisdom that John generously shared with us that spring day in Oregon all those years ago, *plus* all the additional wisdom he has accrued in the years since.

In 2012, the same year I first met John, I wrote a book titled *The Power of Beliefs in Business*. During my research and writing, I came to understand the significant role our beliefs play in shaping our companies. Our beliefs drive our actions. I learned too, for the first time, that beliefs are *not* genetic. They're *all* learned. And if they're learned, they can also be changed. When we change our beliefs, we change our lives.

From Founder to Future is based on a set of beliefs that are very different from those of the mainstream modern-day business world. They are, pretty much across the board, beliefs that we at Zingerman's share with John. First and foremost is the belief that the purpose of a business is to enrich the lives of everyone who's a part of it.

There are, in fact, good alternative business models. Many of them exist on the Main Streets of our country, far from Wall Street, and were created to support, enhance, and embellish this belief. These models—co-ops, employee stock ownership plans (ESOPs), and purpose trusts, to name three—are the subject of *From Founder to Future*. When you finish reading this book, you are almost certain to have a solid sense of some of these well-practiced but rarely discussed options—all the stuff I wish we had known about back in 1982.

In case you are wondering, this alternative set of beliefs can really work. Zingerman's Community of Businesses is one example. In our highly imperfect way, we have pieced together many of the inspiring ideas that John shares in these pages. The little deli that my business partner and I first opened with two staff members is now a community of a dozen different Zingerman's businesses, with over seven hundred staff members and annual sales in excess of $80 million. Over the years, we have created our own crazy hybrid of the things that John writes about. Over 270 of the folks who work here own a share; our twenty-two-person partners group, with worker representation, governs the organization by consensus; we practice servant leadership and open-book management; and all our meetings are open. And, oh yeah—two years ago, we formally rolled out our perpetual purpose trust (which you can learn more about in chapter 2).

Reflecting on all this, I will share my strongly held belief that if this book were required reading in every business school, we could be living in a very different country today. Employee ownership, equity, active citizenship, community focus, and consensus decision-making might well be the norm.

The point of John's work is not for the rest of us to simply copy what they do at South Mountain. Rather, it's to encourage all of us to go out and create our own unique constructs that are well suited to our own particular settings and beliefs. The work of making this kind of community-minded, employee-owned business may not be easy, but it is entirely achievable. Thanks to John's generous sharing in this superb book, that work can now happen far more quickly and successfully! *From Founder to Future* allows us all to educate ourselves so that we too can learn to work more effectively, more generously, and more meaningfully as we make our way through the world.

INTRODUCTION

Five Transitions to Commonwealth

Small businesses can be living systems that work for all the right reasons: to make people's lives more meaningful and satisfying, to spread wealth more equitably, to enhance democracy, to treat the planet and each other better, and to protect mission and purpose. Making work that matters. This book is about reshaping tomorrow's workplace for both individual fulfillment and the common good. Business can be at the heart of the great civilizational shift that we need today.

There are nearly three million US companies whose owners are over age 55 and that qualify as small businesses (defined by the US Small Business Administration as independent businesses with fewer than five hundred employees).[1] By 2040, a "silver tsunami" of baby boomer business owner retirements will have resulted in trillions of dollars in small business assets changing hands.[2] Some of the retiring owners will pass their businesses on to family members or a key employee or two. Some will unceremoniously close the doors.

Others have sufficient value that they might be sold to strategic buyers or private equity. They may be absorbed, bundled, relocated, squeezed, carved up, and "sold for parts." The role of these small businesses as contributors to their communities may end as management without soul takes over, or if they close and leave empty storefronts on Main Street.

But many business owners want to keep their organizations vital, healthy, and independent beyond their personal leadership. They want to preserve the purpose they envisioned and developed over time. At the same time, many employees, as well as young Gen X, millennial, and Gen Z entrepreneurs, are hungry for work that's honest, meaningful, impactful, and inclusive.

Author David Korten explains in *The Great Turning* that "we are slowly making progress as a nation toward achieving liberty and justice for all only through the long and difficult struggles of the excluded."[3] Of those who have been left out, a large segment is the workers who produce our nation's goods and services—a group consisting of people of all colors, genders, persuasions, and national origins. Our economic system directs wealth to owners and shareholders while workers are generally limited to a wage. We could change that. I think we will. Widespread employee ownership may be the platform we stand on to build that change.

Meanwhile, most business owners, financial advisers, accountants, and attorneys (to say nothing of employees) are unaware of the array of unconventional ownership opportunities available to them. My intention is to spread some intelligence, in whatever modest way, about employee ownership and business practice possibilities that could stimulate a thriving new economy that serves people, place, and planet. An economy that works for all.

What if the 32 million-plus employees of the nearly three million companies could purchase these businesses from the retiring owners in creative new ways?[4] Could employee ownership alter the chemistry of our economy and culture and uplift the fortunes of both the entrepreneurs who have built small businesses and the employees who have contributed to their success?

That's my question.

These people, who comprise roughly one-fifth of our nation's workforce, have helped to build these businesses, and their livelihood depends on the stability of their workplaces.[5]

There's a second question: What if ownership does not shift to the employees? What will become of these small businesses that are at the heart of our economy and our communities? If private equity sinks its teeth into these companies, or if no buyer is found and they shut their doors, the livelihoods of these employees—and whole communities and local economies—could be threatened.

From the 1930s to the 1960s, labor unions helped to create a prosperous American middle class by negotiating increasingly higher wages and a host of other benefits for workers. Wealth and income inequality declined significantly.

In 1970, at the end of that period, the average CEO's pay was roughly twenty times the typical worker's pay. It has grown to roughly three hundred times. If worker pay had grown as quickly as CEO pay during the past fifty years, the minimum wage today would be more than \$100/hour.[6]

Nothing like that has happened. Workers have been left behind. Neither the Republican Party or the Democratic Party has delivered. This book proposes that employee ownership is the answer, and that it could reward owners and workers at once, dramatically affect wealth inequality, and sustain valuable businesses for generations to come. And it could help to heal our fractured democracy.

THE FIVE TRANSITIONS

Converting to employee ownership alone is not enough. I hope the stories and information in this book will help business owners, their advisers, and their employees successfully begin to accomplish Five Transitions. Each transition represents a progression—from your business as it is to the business it could be.

- **Ownership:** from proprietary to widely shared and accessible to all
- **Leadership:** from original founder to next generation
- **Mission:** from unprotected to permanent preservation of purpose
- **Management and Governance:** from top-down control to participatory and democratic
- **Impact:** from business-as-usual to certified B Corps force for good

Don't expect to fully achieve all these transitions: few companies have. But you may want to hold them as your intended goalposts, even if it takes decades or generations to get all the way down the field.

The first two transitions—Ownership and Leadership—are the foundations, and each is inevitable as founders grow older and approach retirement. But there are different ways those evolutions could go. Ownership may or may not shift to the employees. Leadership transitions could be carefully thought through or not. We need to plan, steer, and implement these successions in ways that promise long-term success and prosperity.

The other three transitions are optional. In many cases, they may not happen at all. But each of these transitions reinforces the others, and if you attempt to achieve them, you have the opportunity to leave a legacy you can be proud of. Mission protection, participatory management and governance, and B Corp certification fill out the aspirational landscape for the employee-owned companies I advocate.

I invite you to examine, understand, and make these Five Transitions. This is what my colleagues and I did with South Mountain Company, the integrated architecture, building, and solar business I cofounded in 1973 and retired from fifty years later, when second-generation leadership ascended. That experience, coupled with helping and observing other businesses making these successions, has convinced me of the extraordinary value of this approach. Now I'll try to convince you.

To do so, I will tell stories of many companies on the Five Transitions path and examine a variety of employee ownership designs: worker cooperatives, employee stock ownership plans, employee ownership trusts, and some exciting new innovations. We will see how clusters of employee-owned companies are becoming ecosystems of support and amplification. Applying these alternative corporate design concepts, small businesses may contribute to a new era of shared prosperity, social impact, and better lives on a healing planet.

The impact of these Five Transitions may extend beyond business. When employees have a voice and play a role in company governance, they are likely to be attracted to participatory leadership in other settings. Democracy in the workplace can nourish collaboration and cooperation in all walks of life. Widespread employee ownership and empowerment might be an essential ingredient in the human story as it unfolds, by spreading the ethos of civic participation, inclusivity, responsibility, stewardship, servant leadership, and kindness.

THE COMMONWEALTH COMPANY

The term I use for a business that is working on the Five Transitions is a CommonWealth company (common ownership, profits, power, information, and purpose). This term was inspired by my friend Robert Leaver, an "organizational therapist" and master meeting facilitator. In 1995, he published an essay that described the qualities and value of such organizations.[7] These qualities included honoring nature by reducing harmful impacts; shaping healthy, productive, and vibrant workplaces; allowing us to live fully in our communities as citizens who care for others; providing truth and transparency to stakeholders; and making profits that generate wealth for the common good.

CommonWealth companies, as I perceive them, employ constant learning and improvement, with loose steering and control, to create continuity, longevity, resilience, impact, and equity. Have a look at your business right now. Maybe it already shares some of these attributes. Maybe you have been working on the Five Transitions for some time and already embarked on the journey toward CommonWealth. If not, there's no time like the present to focus on this scaffold of purpose and begin to climb its ladder. Start with B Corp certification, then keep going and become a CommonWealth company. Implement the Five Transitions over time to whatever degree you can or wish. You have built something important. It can be even more than you may have imagined.

HONEST WORK

Work can be one of our most important sources of meaning, fulfillment, relationships, learning, growth, creativity, and inspiration. I was fortunate to discover this early and quite by accident. Without intention or plan, I entered the world of business in my youth and found that it satisfied my longings for joy, justice, and impact.

I am lucky—really lucky—to have experienced, for half a century, the kind of work that pulls you out of bed each morning like a powerful magnet. My colleagues and I, in unlikely fashion, with little knowledge and a surplus of naïve enthusiasm, developed South Mountain Company into an emblematic worker co-op. I hope this book will remove the "luck part" for you and replace it with intention.

Maybe this book can provide a new road map for your own journey by proposing an alternative to the way work often is: heartless, exploitative, extractive, and rootless. Employee ownership and the other four transitions are the milestones on the map. Many models that support honest work are available, accessible, practical, and rewarding. They provide a framework for a fundamentally different way to do business in today's world, a way we could call "regenerative," because the seeds of equity and continuity become baked into the organizational DNA. You will read stories of some of these companies in this book.

As your work on the Five Transitions progresses, you will build community in your workplace, deeper connections to the places where you work and live, and greater business success. When the people who are making the decisions share in the rewards from those decisions, and the consequences too, better decisions will surely result for business, community, people, and planet.

EMPLOYEE OWNERSHIP DESIGNS

Of the corporate designs that support Five Transitions ownership and leadership successions, the worker cooperative (co-op) has become one of the silver tsunami succession entities of choice. The appeal of the worker co-op has also spread to younger founders who are not ready to retire but see the value of early employee ownership conversions. Worker co-ops have flown quietly under the radar, even though they exist in all sizes in many parts of the world. They have tremendous potential to spread and prosper here in the United States.

Meanwhile, the employee stock option plan (ESOP) is the most widespread form of US employee ownership; thousands of ESOPs employ roughly 14 million employee-owners nationwide.[8] Highly regulated by Internal Revenue Service (IRS) and Department of Labor rules, ESOPs allow workers to obtain company stock through a trust constructed by company management.

Coming on strong are both the employee ownership trust (EOT), which is relatively unusual in the United States but widespread in Great Britain, and its companion, the perpetual purpose trust (PPT). Patagonia, Zingerman's, and Organically Grown Company are examples of companies who have made highly publicized recent conversions to PPTs.

Underlying this developing new era of purpose-driven business is the B Corp movement. More than eight thousand companies in over ninety countries have undergone the rigorous process of certification to earn the recognition that they are truly honoring a triple bottom line, which means that they focus as much on social and environmental progress as on profits.[9] According to B Lab, the nonprofit network driving this movement, "We won't stop until all business is a force for good."[10]

The Five Transitions to CommonWealth are about business that enhances life and work. This book intends to accelerate the growth of employee ownership models and inclusive business practices and to help us be capable architects as we design the next generation of corporate entities.

This book's message is for every small business, from those just out of the gate to the very mature. Each of these companies should be doing succession planning *right now*. This preparation has tremendous *immediate* benefits— building leadership capacity and an inclusive workplace culture that boosts business efficacy every day. As younger generations raise their voices for authenticity and equity in their work, I hope to strengthen that case and inspire many early conversions and transitions.

The small business silver tsunami offers an unprecedented opportunity to expand wealth creation for workers who have traditionally been underrepresented. In my view, our economy should work for all (which ours currently does not) just as our democratic political system should ensure liberty and justice for all (which ours currently does not). Both aspirations should be among our highest priorities as individuals, as a society, and in business.

THE STORIES IN THIS BOOK

This book has three parts: Building CommonWealth Companies, Employee Ownership Designs, and Implementing the Five Transitions. Additional material and assets that will be useful to companies working on one or more of the Five Transitions are both noted throughout the book and gathered at the end in the Resources section, which includes influential publications and organizations that have helped shape my thinking. A Discussion Guide is provided for use in classrooms and book groups.

My purpose is to bring something I have experienced in my life and my work and share it with other small business owners, workers, and entrepreneurs in a way that is simple, accessible, instructive, and story-based.

The stories I tell of exceptional companies, people, and organizations are anecdotal. Mostly, they come from personal interviews with generous people. As I spoke to people and wrote, something I found particularly inspiring was the shared recognition that there is tremendous momentum in the movement to democratize business and share wealth among those who do the work. The possibilities are thrilling.

To those who should be in these pages and aren't, I say that I see this book as a first iteration. I expect to continue telling these stories long after this book is complete, and I look forward to telling yours.

This storytelling began during two six-month sabbaticals from my work at South Mountain Company in 2004 and 2005, when I wrote *The Company We Keep*; another sabbatical produced a second edition called *Companies We Keep*. It was published in 2008 and is still in print.[11] Seventeen years after its publication, readers still contact me to say that the book has influenced their business journey. When I say that I think of it as ancient and out-of-date, they often reply, "No, it's timeless." I hope this book will feel that way to you.

YOU AND ME

I welcome this opportunity to explore with you the possibilities of building the business environment we aspire to rather than accepting the dysfunctional status quo to which we will otherwise continue to subject ourselves. You have a unique opportunity to leave behind a legacy of value as a compelling business movement gains momentum. This book is about companies, commerce, and the people who do the great work of using business to improve their lives and the lives of others. I hope to launch you on a Five Transitions journey to Common-Wealth. Let's walk this path together.

If you have questions, comments, criticisms, or ideas to share, I would enjoy hearing from you at john@abramsangell.com, and you can access the *Companies We Keep* blog at abramsangell.com/blog.

BUILDING COMMONWEALTH COMPANIES

This first part of the book sets our stage.

Chapter 1 tells the story of the company I know best, South Mountain Company, which I inadvertently cofounded when I was twenty-three years old. There was no plan. At the time, I had no sense of the meaning of business. I only knew that I wanted to do the work I had come to love and hoped to share the experience with others. If an all-knowing future gazer had told me back then what the company would become fifty years later, I would not have known what they were talking about. It was a learn-as-you-go, build-the-road-as-you-travel endeavor.

Chapter 2 explores the difficulties of preserving company purpose and finding opportunities to codify mission and create impact in your company. It describes some of the characteristics of triple-bottom-line businesses and their relation to common current economic practice. Three stories of exemplary companies—Dean's Beans, Snow River, and Zingerman's—are used to demonstrate the meaning of the Five Transitions to CommonWealth.

CHAPTER 1

MAKING A MOUNTAIN

When I entered college in 1967, the Vietnam War was raging and America's youth were outraged. On a sunny October day, I joined a hundred thousand others at the Lincoln Memorial in Washington, DC, for the largest antiwar protest to date. Many of us marched on to the Pentagon, which was ringed with soldiers bearing rifles. We put flowers in the barrels. Occasionally, a soldier would throw down his rifle and join the cheering crowd.

Meanwhile, the back-to-the-land movement was picking up steam. Young people were moving to rural America to learn the skills of self-sufficiency and to invent a future different from the one we were raised to expect. I never finished college because the insistent pull of this current drew me in hook, line, and sinker.

This migration became my higher education. Stewart Brand's *Whole Earth Catalog* was my primary textbook for learning and skill-building.[1] In its pages, and in the rural outbacks of Vermont, Northern California, Oregon, and British Columbia, I inadvertently found a path to a fulfilling career that began by making crude houses and fixing dilapidated ones. In those days, I was more at home in America's agrarian past than in mainstream society's present.

In 1973, I started a woodworking company with two partners in upstate New York. Several years later, one of them, Mitchell Posin, left with me for Martha's Vineyard, an island off the south coast of Massachusetts. We went there planning to build a house, make some money, and head back to Vermont in six months. A year later, we were still toiling away on this handmade house, and the money was gone. But the results were reasonably good, and others asked us to make houses for them. Several years later, we were still at it. An older friend and mentor of mine appreciated our work. One day, while we were showing him a house in progress, he said, "Beautiful, beautiful work . . . just splendid." And then, "Are you making any money?"

"No," I chuckled, "we seem to lose money on every project we do."

"Well, Abrams," he said, "You've got a unique idea. Subsidized housing for the rich."

That bombshell inspired me to learn about business—what it is, how you do it, and what it can mean for our communities and our world (and how to make subsidized housing for those who need it!).

I was twenty-seven years old when my friend Lee delivered that blunt assessment. My passion for business grew. In 1978, we were lucky to have a client who said, "You have to make a profit on this house, but I'm not willing to pay more than I should. So, I'm going to teach you how to make a profit." He did. I shuffled paper, created systems, hired a bookkeeper, and gave the same respect to my spreadsheets as I did to my chisels. I learned that business is a craft just like making a staircase. My partner Mitchell left to become a farmer, and the company became a sole proprietorship.

The only real job I've ever had for more than six months was at South Mountain Company.[2] There, I learned from books, targeted classwork, and a network of peers about carpentry and woodworking, design, high-performance building, and renewable energy. I hired and managed staff, conducted sales, guided clients, and drew up estimates and contracts. I dove all the way into my studies and read extensively about small-business practice, mission-driven business, and the philosophy of a triple bottom line, a term that would not exist until business writer John Elkington invented it in 1994.[3]

I learned to do these things entirely by the seat of my pants, mostly in a half-baked way—just well enough to know how to attract others who could do them better than I.

I learned about affordable housing—how to fund it, how to make it, and how to make it better. I cultivated the skills of community activism—how to facilitate meetings and processes to make social change. I applied my learning to our work at South Mountain and shared it with other companies and communities.

SHARING OWNERSHIP

In 1986, South Mountain Company (SMCo) was thirteen years old with a dozen employees. Two of those employees who had been with me the longest, Steve Sinnett and Pete Ives, came to talk to me. "We don't want to take the usual path of moving on and starting our own businesses," they said. "We want to stay and make our careers here. But we need more of a stake than an hourly wage." I could easily have made my two friends minor partners, but it occurred to us that if we did our job well, this situation would manifest over and over in the years to come. The three of us wanted to imagine a structure that would consistently welcome new partners into ownership.

We did not have to imagine. Early investigations revealed the worker co-op. At the time there were few, but those we found were inspiring. A hinge point was my embrace of the idea of converting from a sole proprietorship to a worker co-op. For a while I was *unhinged*—alternately frightened and excited by our deliberations. I had the power and the greatest financial and emotional investment; therefore, I had the most to lose. Sometimes, during those sessions, it felt like I was tugging on the reins of a runaway horse. I was concerned that my customary freedom to act solo might be constrained by shared ownership. What if the thing I've built with painstaking care and love evolves into something I no longer like? But the potential for shared responsibility and ownership to provide new freedom for me and new potential for the company was a potent mix that drove me forward.

We hired Peter Pitegoff, an attorney at the Industrial Cooperatives Association, now known as the ICA Group, to advise us. On January 1, 1987, we reorganized as a worker co-op. Over time, it became clear that my fears were unfounded—I came to love it more. Today, nearly four decades later, SMCo is an integrated architecture, building, and solar energy company with a highly democratic workplace thriving under second-generation leadership.

Why did my two friends want to stay? And how is this relevant to the choices that face so many small businesses?

I think they sensed that they could continue to grow the cultural seeds that had been planted in rich soil—rewarding work, deep collaboration, exceptional quality, long-term service, comradery, friendship, community engagement, and shared equity—and that they didn't need to try to re-create that elsewhere.

SMCo has delivered on its promise—people have stayed and fashioned successful careers. Between 2010 and 2022, nine employee-owners retired after long SMCo careers, during which they accumulated financial equity. (Their average length of employment was thirty-two years.) Another longtime cohort replaced those employee-owners and has assumed the mantle of current leadership. A dedicated, passionate group of younger employee-owners is beginning to form the core of future third-generation leadership.

THE SABBATICALS

A key part of building South Mountain's ownership culture was our progression from my full operational leadership to distributed collaborative and democratic management. That path began in 2003 and 2004, when I took two six-month sabbaticals to write a book and see how the company would fare. Before I left, we did intensive planning to devise a management system for my absence. The plan was a flop. Nothing catastrophic happened; it just didn't work, and people were unhappy. Morale tanked. When I returned, we spent another six months analyzing what had gone wrong, planning anew, and I left again. This time, there was traction. It was the beginning of true shared management at SMCo.

An important element of building the ownership culture at South Mountain has been the policy of hiring "future owners" as opposed to just hiring employees. Skills can be taught; character cannot. The development of this concept has led to a thorough and deliberate hiring process that acknowledges that newly employed people may want to stay with the company for their entire careers. It's important that the process "gets the right people on the bus," as author Jim Collins said in his book *Good to Great*.[4]

The arc of the SMCo adventure—from its countercultural roots to worker co-op transition to next-generation leadership—continues and strengthens. It has not been a journey without struggle and stress. In his book *Decolonizing Wealth*, Edgar Villanueva says, "The role for leaders is to create a safe space for vulnerability by sharing their own trauma and grief and by modeling listening, compassion, and empathy. These developments are part of the shift toward enabling people to bring their full selves to work."[5]

I only fully learned this essential truth late in my career, thirty-five years after SMCo began. I regret that it took me so long. I thought I needed to model competence and optimism and protect my colleagues from distress. But sharing the burden is equally important, and I underestimated the degree to which others would rise up and engage when faced with major difficulties.

Until 2008.

TESTING THE SOUL OF SOUTH MOUNTAIN

The economic crash of 2008 was a shock to the system that shook our company to the core. For years, every SMCo employee had come to work each day with productive work to do. Now, a deluge of crushing cancellations and postponements untethered us from the comfort we had known. It became a year of trials and tribulations. But difficulty and opportunity mingle; at times, it is hard to distinguish one from the other. The author Andre Gide relates the experience of a trip he took into the Belgian Congo in 1925:

> My party had been pushing ahead at a fast pace for a number of days, and one morning when we were ready to set out, my native bearers, who carried the food and equipment, were found sitting about without any preparations made for starting the day. Upon being questioned, they said, quite simply, that they had been traveling so fast that they had gotten ahead of their souls and were going to stay quietly in camp for the day for their souls to catch up with them. So, they came to a complete stop.[6]

At SMCo, we did not have the luxury of coming to a complete stop, but we needed to make time "for our souls to catch up with us" during this period of reckoning.

Along with considering how to rebuild our vanished work backlog, it was our moment to tackle the unthinkable: What happens when the day comes that there is not enough work for all? The examination had surprising results.

There were five important components of the inquiry that ensued:

* contending with the likelihood of work shortages;
* communicating with employees consistently and transparently;

- evaluating the state of the company;
- thinking differently about our work: type, location, and mission satisfaction; and
- conscious, proactive marketing and messaging.

Work Shortages

Deep, heartfelt discussions led to a company policy stipulating that if there was not enough work to provide full-time employment for all individuals in the company, management will enact the following measures, in this order:

1. Implement voluntary temporary rolling furloughs.
2. Employ people to do speculative (income deferred) work.
3. Employ people to do non-income-producing work (just to keep them working).
4. Strategically reduce hours worked.
5. Reduce wages across the board by a percentage.
6. Implement involuntary temporary rolling furloughs.

The thrilling part was that never during these difficult discussions did the word "layoffs" come up. That would have been a simple solution, but nobody suggested it.

Ultimately, we used each of the six work shortage strategies at one time or another. I will never forget the company meeting at which we announced that we were cutting all wages, across the board, by 20 percent. Several employees came up to me afterward and expressed appreciation, right after their wages were cut by 20 percent! Their gratitude was for a culture of mutual support and the fact that those who earned the most were losing the most. This was a time of workplace community rather than a time of fragmentation and protection of individual self-interests.

Communication

Constant communication made these difficult times less so. We used written memos and all-company meetings to express the state-of-the-business in detail. Everyone had opportunities to react. Good information, we learned, is essential, especially in difficult times. The more people know, the less they need to worry about, imagine, or make up. And the more they can contribute to solutions.

Evaluation

We engaged in a rigorous assessment of our strengths and weaknesses and came to two hard-to-swallow conclusions that existed regardless of our economic situation:

- some people were in the wrong jobs, and we were unable to find the right jobs for them;
- some people were not carrying their weight, and we were unable to sufficiently help them thrive and grow.

Ultimately, we realized that we had to reduce the size of the company *even if we didn't absolutely need to.* Five long-time employees (two of them owners) were ushered to retirement or new, more suitable careers with significant assistance and large severances.

We were not pleased with what we had to do, but we were proud of the process that led to it and the way it was conducted. Difficult as it was— wounding, wrenching, and heartbreaking—the risk of complacency was clearly greater than the risk of acting.

Rebuilding

Evaluating personnel and taking action to make a leaner and smarter company was a step in the right direction, but we also had to rebuild the company by undertaking several initiatives:

- We expanded the breadth of our work by moving into institutional work and accepting several mission-aligned projects off the island (previously, we had been committed to limiting our work to our small island region).
- We assumed the risk of financing, building, and selling our first house on speculation, to create work at a time when it was needed.
- We created a solar business that would soon become an essential part of SMCo—it extended our mission and balanced our workload.

■ We corralled our resources and began to build a reserve fund that would be there when the next economic crisis came (which turned out to be something we could not have predicted—a pandemic).

Our ability to successfully tackle this tremendous challenge was a result of the shared-ownership muscle we built in prior years. During the COVID-19 pandemic, we were again able to successfully traverse tough new terrain. Our response to 2008 led to a new maturity that will serve the company well in times of duress in the future, too.

MAPPING THE FUTURE

At the end of 2010, we were worn out and smarting but excited and ready for the journey ahead. Our souls had caught up with us. The work rolled in, we rolled with it, and normalcy returned. Looking back, I now know that the crash of 2008 was the second-best thing that ever happened to us (our worker co-op transition was the first). Our response to the crash did more than solve problems. It evolved into an ongoing process of intensive culture-building and constant examination that has made the company stronger.

With the crisis behind us and new company capacity, it became possible to consider major initiatives beyond day-to-day business. Strategic planning and the creation of five- and ten-year plans led us to legacy considerations. I was now the sixty-one-year-old leader. What kind of future could we envision for the company after my tenure?

FROM AVALANCHE SCENARIO TO TRANSITION PLAN

I'm an avid skier, so it's not unreasonable to ask, "What happens tomorrow if I'm buried in an avalanche today?" So, in 2014, SMCo began to consider long-term continuity by creating our first avalanche scenario. In 2019, after five years of intermittent updates, we completed the design of a leadership transition plan. We gave ourselves three years to conduct intensive capacity-building and preparations for the transition. At the end of 2022, I would be seventy-three years old and ready to move on and yield to the next generation of SMCo leaders.

As we developed our succession plan, we found a particularly compelling model at King Arthur Baking Company, an emblematic Vermont business. In

1999, the first nonfamily CEO, Steve Voigt, was hired. In 2004, the Sands family, which had owned the company for two hundred years, sold it to the employees, and King Arthur became an employee stock ownership plan (ESOP). After Voigt led the company for fifteen years, he retired, and three of his leadership team took over as co-CEOs, an unusual structure.

At South Mountain, we never imagined hiring a new CEO from outside. We had a strong leadership team, but no single person stood out as the obvious next CEO, so the King Arthur model intrigued us. We spoke to the new co-leaders at King Arthur about why they did it that way, what was gained, and how it was working. It seemed like a good fit for us. The five members of our leadership team had complementary skills, characters, and interests. Four of them were department directors, and the chief operating officer at the time, Deirdre Bohan, had been comanaging the company with me ever since my sabbaticals. Her job had been *like* a co-CEO, but she always maintained that she was not the person to be the sole CEO. But five co-CEOs? That seemed unworkable. The answer became clear: Deirdre should be the CEO in a first-among-equals collaborative arrangement with the leadership team.

I proposed this at a leadership meeting after discussing the idea with Deirdre. I expected some pushback or resentment from those who might have expected to be one of the co-CEOs, but there was none. Everyone recognized the impracticality of five people sharing CEO responsibilities. Most importantly, everyone had great confidence in Deirdre's suitability for this position. Over twenty-eight years at South Mountain, as she progressed from bookkeeper to interior designer to COO to comanager, she became a dedicated, skillful, and compassionate leader. Although she never aspired to the CEO position and for years had made it clear she would not be comfortable with it, this time it had become as obvious to her as it was to the rest of us that she was the right choice.

On November 19, 2019, at our annual company-wide Day of Business meeting, we unveiled the transition plan. It was a threshold moment.

THE SUCCESSION

By this time, SMCo enjoyed the good fortune of having thirty-five employees who could skillfully design, build, engineer, practice finance, administer, and manage. And while very few of them came to South Mountain with significant leadership expertise, many came with a leadership orientation, and they developed those skills as we conducted a rigorous process of leadership development in preparation for my retirement. Our hiring practices had brought the right people onto the bus.

In December 2022, I retired from the company I founded when I was twenty-three years old. I relinquished ownership and the titles of president and CEO and became founder and president emeritus.

I had only one personal goal for the transition adventure: to leave the company that I deeply love in the best shape it has ever been, ready to go forward. And to leave the people in this company, who I deeply love as well, in a position to succeed.

Max De Pree, the founder of Herman Miller, says in his book *Leadership Is an Art,* "The first responsibility of a leader is to define reality. The last is to say thank you. In between the two, the leader must become a servant."[7]

My last act as leader of South Mountain was to say thank you to everyone in the company from whom I had learned so much. Without their extraordinary commitment and humanity, I would not have been able to be me, and the company would not have been what it had become.

The particulars of the South Mountain leadership transition are detailed in chapter 10.

COMPLETION AND TWO YEARS LATER

Two years later, I can say unequivocally that South Mountain is not the company that I built by the seat of my worn and faded Levi's; it's the company that new leadership is guiding into uncharted terrain, using tools, methods, and information barely imaginable a decade or two ago.

People invariably ask me what it feels like to have stepped away from this significant anchor of my identity. Here's the best way I can explain it: I used to think I had the finest job in the world because I was able to do the work I love in the ways I wished. But for many years, my job was primarily to respond and react, to do what was asked of me, to limit errors to the non-catastrophic, and to carry great responsibility—essentially, to satisfy the expectations of others and to help them thrive. My job was to be an effective servant leader. It *was* as good as it gets—I loved it every day—but I see it differently from my new perch.

Only now do I have the freedom of a no-expectations work life. A fresh start. I need this freedom in the same way that the new South Mountain leadership needs theirs—they must lead in *their* way as I have stepped *out* of the way. I deeply miss the extraordinary people at SMCo as my involvement has diminished, but I do not miss the burden of responsibility. After 50 years, it had become like gravity—I never entirely recognized its presence—but I now emphatically feel its absence. As I write, the first two years of South Mountain without me— and me without South Mountain—have ended. The emotional part is probably more poignant on my side; occasionally, I get homesick. It truly was my second home for half a century.

Meanwhile, fifty years after its inauspicious beginnings, the company endures with its structure strong, its forward motion palpable, and its embedded spirit intact.

BUILDING A CATHEDRAL

In a way, South Mountain's development was like building a cathedral. Irish business philosopher Charles Handy gives this perspective:

Cathedrals inspire. It is not only their grandeur or splendor, but the thought that they often took more than fifty years to build. Those who designed them, those who first worked on them, knew for certain that they would never see them finished. They knew only that they were creating something glorious which would stand for centuries, long after their own names had been forgotten. They had their own dream of the sublime and of immortality. We may not need any more cathedrals, but we do need cathedral thinkers, people who can think beyond their own lifetimes.[8]

The cathedral is not literal. The SMCo cathedral is fundamentally different from those that were built in the Middle Ages in a feudal and theocratic society that extracted wealth from the land and human labor and concentrated it in the church. Ours is a cathedral of sharing, kindness, and equity.

I can tell you how the cathedral metaphor evolved for me. Early on, I fell in love with the crafts of building and business, and with the people I practiced with. I wanted that to last. To fulfill its ambitions, South Mountain has become a

CommonWealth company that tries to serve stakeholders' needs in exemplary ways. In return, those people care for the structure and maintain it over time.

The journey goes on, driven by love for the human potential embedded in the enterprise. It took all of fifty years to cross the Five Transitions threshold. You may be able to do it in less time. You may not. It doesn't really matter. The engagement in the process makes the difference, not how far you get or how long it takes.

Although South Mountain is not the main subject of this book, it is the foundation and will often play a role in this story. It is an example of the kind of enterprise that I celebrate here, and I hope it resonates with you.

CHAPTER 2

MISSION-DRIVEN ENTERPRISE

On April 11, 2000, after a mighty struggle and against the wishes of cofounder and CEO Ben Cohen and other company leaders, Ben and Jerry's Homemade was forced by law to sell the premier socially oriented firm in America to multinational Unilever. It was a momentous wake-up call in socially responsible business circles, where maintaining purpose and mission suddenly became a serious issue.

In his book *Ice Cream Social*, Brad Edmundson writes that "Ben, Jerry, and [board chair] Jeff Furman were exhausted and heartbroken. In a 2008 interview with the *Guardian*, Jerry said, 'We did not want to sell the business. But we were a public company, and the Board of Directors' legal responsibility was to maximize shareholder value. It was extremely difficult, heart-wrenching. It was a horrible experience.'"[1]

Ben and Jerry's is a gold standard for business social activism. Behind all their efforts was a vision they called "linked prosperity"—the simple but radical idea that when the company prospers, everything and everybody it touches should prosper too: employees, suppliers, customers, communities, and the environment. And although they were forced to sell, they negotiated a deal with Unilever that injected this social mission into one of the world's largest corporations. Says Edmundson, "A small socially responsible company had written the essential noneconomic elements of its mission statement into a contract, had insisted that the contract be perpetual, and had persuaded a much larger company to sign that contract before agreeing to sell."[2]

Would it have been better if Ben and Jerry's had been able to remain private? It's hard to say. Their social impact work may have affected the much-larger publicly traded Unilever in many positive ways due to the strength of the agreement, which preserved the social mission, operational autonomy, and an independent Ben and Jerry's board to safeguard the company's values and practices. A model was created that other companies under pressure from large buyers have been able to use. It was a battle that launched an experiment to keep mission intact in business.

B LAB, B CORP, AND BENEFIT CORPORATIONS

Ben and Jerry's expressive concept of "linked prosperity" never became commonplace, but the ice cream activists were an inspiration for the establishment of B Lab, the organization that invented two influential mission-driven business ideas: benefit corporations and certified B Corps.[3] Benefit corporations have become new legal entities in forty-one states and eight countries, and certified B Corps have become a worldwide embodiment of the linked prosperity concept.

The two schemes originated with three college roommates—Jay Coen Gilbert, Bart Houlihan, and Andy Kassoy—who had been searching for a way to be of greatest service to social justice. The "B" stands for benefit. As a community, certified B Corps are building a new sector of the economy in which the race to the top isn't to be the best *in* the world but to be the best *for* the world.

A certified B Corp (commonly known as a B Corp) is a designation that "a business is meeting high standards of verified performance, accountability, and transparency on factors from employee benefits and charitable giving to supply chain practices and input materials."[4] It derives from a rigorous, documented assessment and scoring system across the three bottom lines—people, planet, and profit. To achieve certification, a company must earn a minimum score of 80 points (out of 200) on the B Impact Assessment. All certified B Corps must share their B Impact report (the summary of their scores) publicly on B Lab's website. Each report is there for all to see. Transparency builds trust.

Companies from different industries that focus on making a positive social and environmental impact have met the B Corp standards and become certified. Among them are: Ben and Jerry's, Patagonia, Eileen Fisher, Seventh Generation, and Dr. Bronner's. For some years, South Mountain Company was the world's highest-scoring B Corp (now it's Dr. Bronners), which always made me skeptical, because that meant we scored higher than a company like Patagonia, which on any given Monday morning does more good for the world than SMCo does in a year of Tuesdays.

Ryan Honeyman, coauthor of *The B Corp Handbook*, says, "The rigor of the B Corp certification process means that it takes serious dedication to complete, which helps to filter out businesses that are not truly committed to meeting the high standards. The result is a passionate, highly innovative group of some of the most socially and environmentally conscious businesses on the planet."[5]

Benefit Corporations

Being a *certified B Corp* is an optional act that can lapse at any time. This is different from being a *benefit corporation*, which is a legal framework (also conceived of by B Lab) that allows companies to pursue social and environmental goals without risking challenges for failing to maximize shareholder profit. Maryland became the first state to pass benefit corporation legislation in 2010. By 2024, forty US states and Washington, DC, had enacted Benefit Corporation legislation, and it had spread to other countries as well.

To comply with this designation a company must change its articles of incorporation to express a commitment to public benefit and higher standards of purpose, transparency, and accountability. It must comply with annual reporting requirements to demonstrate its beneficial actions. The political work that has produced these laws is one of the great achievements of B Lab.

B Corp Troubles

But all is not peaches and cream in the B Corp world.

In 2023, the managing editor of the *Financial Times*, Anjli Raval, wrote that as B Corp begins to attract attention from large multinationals, some of the smaller companies feel that the standards may be eroding, with the focus shifting to getting multinationals to be "less bad" rather than "transformationally good."[6]

My personal experience is that B Lab has always been an organization committed to learning and evolving. When South Mountain first certified in the early days of B Corp, we noticed that the certification process did not award any points for employee ownership. We pointed this out to the B Corp founders. Their immediate reaction was, "Wow—huge oversight on our part." They corrected the omission.

But criticism continues. In a 2024 BBC article, author Elizabeth Bennett says:

> The backlash hit fever pitch in 2022, when a group of B Corp-certified coffee companies alongside Portland, Oregon-based non-profit Fair World Project, wrote an open letter to B Lab Global as Nestlé-owned coffee company Nespresso received its B Corp designation in April of that year. Calling out Nespresso's "abysmal track record on human rights" and "extractive business model," they asked for stricter standards across B Lab Global.[7]

Curious about these substantive criticisms levied on an organization and a process that I admire, I wanted to find out more. I spoke to several people. The first was Jay Coen-Gilbert, one of the founders of B Lab and a primary architect of the certification process and builder of its implementation. Jay left B Lab in 2020 to pursue new work with anti-racism and justice. I asked him whether the criticisms are warranted. "Some are valid," he told me. "And I'd say they're helpful. They're a feature, not a bug. If we're humble enough to recognize that no standards are perfect and we're all doing this in the spirit of continuous improvement, then we should be grateful, not defensive, when folks point out deficiencies or errors, and we should adapt and improve."

B Lab has responded to the current criticism with a change in standards. B Corp certification processes are now tailored to a company's size and complexity, with larger, more complex companies being required to meet more rigorous standards and undergo deeper verification processes. The bigger your business is, the harder it is to become a certified B Corp.

In a March 2024 email, Sarah Schwimmer, the current co-lead executive of B Lab Global, the organization that oversees B Corp certification worldwide, explained it to me this way:

We benefit from having a community that is diverse, and that includes a range of industries and companies of different sizes. It makes us that much more credible and powerful as a movement to show that many kinds of companies can improve their positive impact and accountability. As we evolve the standards, we encourage B Corps who see room for improvement to participate. For our next iteration, we've engaged more than a thousand stakeholders in each of two rounds of consultation. We are confident that the new standards will serve as a galvanizing and unifying force for our community as it continues to grow in influence and impact.

Next, I spoke to Ryan Honeyman and Shawn Berry, two of the partners at LIFT Economy, an impact consulting firm whose mission is to "create, model, and share a racially just, regenerative, and locally self-reliant economy that works for the benefit of all life."[8] They run a highly successful Next Economy MBA course for entrepreneurs, and they are among the many consultants who help companies with the complex process of B Corp certification.

But they are in no way starry-eyed about what B Corp certification means. Shawn explained, "We present B Corp certification as wholly inadequate to get to an economy that truly works for all. As we help companies to certify, our position is okay, hey, you made it past the 80-point threshold [the average certification score is in the range of 83], but now that you're certified, let's go to 200. Let's push to the top end of this thing. Certification is just a foot in the door because *barely certified* is not super impactful."

But even if getting to 80 is a low bar, it's still very challenging. Since B Lab's inception, over 200,000 companies have used the B Impact Assessment to measure their impact but only approximately four percent have managed to achieve certification.

Good Business for All

It's clear that B Corp certification is an important positive step toward good business. B Corps are using business to make lasting social, political, and environmental change and create meaningful work that empowers those who do it every day.

As I've said, it's not easy to get certification in the first place, and each company must recertify every three years and show improvement. For very small businesses that have little administrative capacity, it can be daunting. You might take a look and say, "This just isn't for us." But digesting the criteria, going through the application process, and taking advantage of B Corp resources is time well spent, even if it doesn't lead directly to certification. That can come when you're ready, if that time comes.

For the millions of small businesses transitioning from founders to future, B Corp designation is a framework that gives verified credibility to a mission-driven enterprise in its quest for corporate, environmental, social, and governance responsibility.

Another business certification program, called JUST, was introduced in 2014 by the International Living Futures Institute (ILFI). Like B Corps, JUST organizations commit to equitable and healthy workplaces, and the (less intensive) certification process examines business policies, practice, and culture. To date, JUST is mostly focused on the architecture and building industries.

CHALLENGING THE GOSPEL OF GROWTH

One thing neither B Corp nor JUST certification addresses is that common business practice suffers from an unshakable allegiance to growth. Our current economic system encourages an almost religious devotion to a more-is-better mentality. Most ecologists—and economists, too—know that the planet cannot sustain perpetual global growth, but the importance of individual enterprise growth is rarely challenged. Business literature neglects the advantages of size optimization. In fact, conventional wisdom implies that small businesses just haven't had greater success yet. Nothing could be further from the truth.

In *Let My People Go Surfing*, Patagonia founder Yves Chouinard says this:

We don't want to be a big company. We want to be the best company, and it's easier to try to be the best small company than the best big company. We must practice self-control. Growth in one part of the company may have to be sacrificed to allow growth in another. It's also important that we have a clear idea of what the limits are to this "experiment" and live within those limits, knowing that the sooner we expand outside them, the sooner the type of company we want will die.[9]

Our view of business is shaped by public corporations that not only are schooled by Wall Street to grow or die but also hold as their purpose the maximization of shareholder—not stakeholder—value. The people who build the company get little, the leaders and investors get most, and income inequality and wealth supremacy result.

But our inquiry need not be about growth versus no growth; it better serves us to think about the quality of growth. Some things we want to grow and some we do not. We want to grow our responsiveness, our satisfaction, our effectiveness, our reputation, our legacy, our relevance, the quality of our products, and our contributions to good lives for our employees and our community. We do not want to grow our waste, our pollution, our unaccounted-for externalities, our unfulfilled commitments, our stress levels, or our client and customer dissatisfactions.

In *Small Giants*, Bo Burlingham profiled fourteen companies for whom mission has been more important than size. The book spawned the Small Giants Community, which now consists of hundreds of purpose-driven companies that trade secrets and create educational opportunities. Growth is not their primary purpose. *Purposeful* growth is. Many embrace "enough."

Opportunities for development without growth are abundant. Through dedication to constant improvement, companies can get better without getting bigger, and they can endure and serve with a commitment to long-term thinking. Millions of small private businesses do not grow much, if at all, and they don't die, either. In fact, they're often quite healthy.

I am not suggesting that every workplace should be modest in scale. But excessive growth may limit good things like invention, personal fulfillment, and the overall quality of workplace culture and products. Most people I talk to want these good things in their work but find it hard to resist the tug of other, more persistent, forces. We tend to think growth is the only path to greater profits and influence and greater well-being, too.

There's a story about a fisherman who was sitting on the beach with his wife one afternoon, enjoying the surf and the sun after a big catch that morning. A wealthy business entrepreneur heard about his success and approached him.

"Why didn't you keep fishing and bring in twice as much?" he asked.

"Why?" said the fisherman.

"Because you could make more money. Maybe buy another boat and hire some employees."

"Why?" the fisherman asked again.

"You could keep growing, increase profits, and buy more boats. If you worked long and hard at it, after some years you'd grow rich."

"Why would I want to do that?"

"Because then you and your wife could retire and relax on the beach," said the business entrepreneur.

"But that's what I'm doing now," said the fisherman.

Sometimes, enough is enough. Dean's Beans is a business that exemplifies the notion of "enough."

DEAN'S BEANS

While working as an environmental and Indigenous rights lawyer in the 1980s, Dean Cycon founded the nonprofit Coffee Kids to improve the lives and livelihoods of coffee-farming families. He soon decided that charity was not enough to bring meaningful change to the people who grow the beans that become the coffee we drink. In 1993, he founded Dean's Beans Organic Coffee to make a for-profit, fair-trade specialty coffee company as a vehicle for social, economic, and environmental change.

Dean wanted to build a successful business that could do more to help the growers and their communities while creating living-wage jobs in the depressed central Massachusetts town of Orange. He wanted to treat employees with the utmost respect, pay them well, provide top-notch benefits, and practice his own seat-of-the-pants form of intuitive open-book management.

He and his colleagues have completed and continue to engage in an extraordinary array of development projects in the coffee-growing regions. Dean says, "We're trying to change the terms of international trade by making true partnerships with primary producers. Change isn't about the goods; it's about people changing when cooperative collaboration becomes embedded in communities."[10]

But as he approached age 70 and wanted to focus his life on writing and activism, he wondered what to do with his beloved business. After years seeking solutions, he had gotten nowhere. "People wanted to buy it," says Dean, "but they were more interested in money than the welfare of the employees and the farmers." Dean wasn't interested in growth—he believed in "enough" and cared about the business's mission, not about getting his coffee into Trader Joe's.

Enter Beth Spong. A mission-driven consultant and longtime nonprofit leader, she was hired by Dean to help with workflow, process improvements, and team alignment. Later he said to her, "I want you to project-manage my transition to retirement."

She accepted the challenge. About the same time, Dean realized he could sell the thriving $6.5 million business to his fifteen employees. "Who better to carry on the mission than the folks who've been doing it all these years?" he said. "Some of them have been here twenty years."

But they needed leadership. During one conversation, Beth heard herself say, "You should hire me to run the company." Until that moment, the thought had never crossed her mind, but as they discussed it, she realized she was ready for "a left turn in my life."[11] Beth became full-time chief operating officer with the understanding that she would become CEO of the new employee-owned entity if all went according to plan.

It did. In mid-2023, the transition was complete; the company is now owned by the employees who helped to build it. Dean remains on the board for three years; other than that, he's mainly a valuable sounding board for Beth.

SMALL IS BEAUTIFUL

Sometimes, like in Dean's case, "enough" is the answer: enough profits to retain and share, enough compensation for all, enough benefits, enough community impact, enough time to give work the attention it deserves, enough communication, enough to manage, enough screwups.

Scale is important, but getting to scale does not have to be about individual company growth. In chapters 5 and 8, I share stories of the ways that employee ownership ecosystems and networks have been able to scale good business without prioritizing individual enterprise growth.

Half a century ago, British economist E. F. Schumacher's classic book *Small Is Beautiful* predicted that the push for endless growth is doomed to fail. His book influenced a generation of social entrepreneurs who operate on the "enough" principle and who emphasize quality over quantity and equity over exclusivity. *Small Is Beautiful* anticipated, in 1973, the problems of a global economy that didn't even exist then. He recommended local control rather than large corporate entities and celebrated the use of "appropriate technology," a phrase that became widespread in the 1970s and refers to technology that is local, environmentally sound, and promotes self-sufficiency. The term has largely been replaced today by "localization," a movement that is stronger than ever and characterized by local commerce, food, and energy production.

When I first read *Small Is Beautiful* in 1974, it fully resonated with the back-to-the-land practices we had explored in prior years, but I had no idea then how influential it would become in the business I was just beginning to build. Schumacher named something that many of us were unknowingly practicing. The principle of "enough" influenced South Mountain when we decided to limit our work to our small region. That decision was accompanied by a commitment to increase our impact by sharing our learning with people and companies beyond our shores rather than by making a larger company with a larger service area.

I recently reread *Small Is Beautiful*. If Schumacher were here today, I believe our propensity to inflict lasting harm on our planet and allow wealth supremacy to reign would have been heartbreaking—but not surprising—to him. On the other hand, Schumacher would have been inspired and uplifted by the ascendance of counterforces like regenerative agriculture, distributed renewable energy, employee ownership, fair trade, and local economic emphasis (Main Street, not Wall Street). He would have appreciated the way the internet allows us to think globally and act locally. He would have loved B Corp, too.

THE HUNDRED-YEAR COMPANY

Kevin Kelly, founding editor of *Wired* magazine, wrote *Excellent Advice for Living* to tell his children the things he has learned that he wishes he could have told them when they were growing up. In it he says, "Bad things can happen fast but almost all good things happen slowly."[12]

Things that last have special qualities that cause them to endure. Think for a moment about the traits of those who live to a very old age, transition to elder-hood, and share the accumulated wisdom of a lifetime. Or consider the two-thousand-year-old redwood trees that create entire embodied ecologies after once having been ordinary trees in their youth.

Even some design innovations take time. Asked by a curious admirer whether the design for the iconic Eames lounge chair came to him in a flash, Charles Eames famously replied, "Yes, sort of a thirty-year flash."

When we build a business, we have the opportunity to build a legacy, not just a money machine. Creation confers responsibility.

Thinking of your company as one that will last a hundred years or more can inspire better business that makes better lives and stronger communities. Most hundred-year companies are driven more by their mission than by money.

Snow River in rural Wisconsin is an example. On the verge of closing in 2019, its conversion to a worker cooperative has been instrumental in preserving community in a small region.

SNOW RIVER

Courtney Berner is the executive director of the University of Wisconsin (UW) Center for Cooperatives, which has been responsible for multiple worker co-op conversions. One that particularly touches her heart is Snow River.

"Snow River is a 125-year-old company in a small rural community north of Green Bay," she said. "Many have worked at this factory with good union jobs for thirty years. Suddenly, in 2019, the owner said, 'I'm out of here. I want to go live in Florida or do whatever I want to do before I die.' He wasn't interested in legacy or the workers."

Snow River is located in Crandon, the county seat of Forest County, which doesn't have a single traffic light or parking meter. The highly profitable com-pany manufactures quality bowls and cutting boards from repurposed wood. Faced with losing their jobs in this area where good jobs are scarce, the employ-ees turned to their union, which knew about worker co-ops and suggested em-ployee ownership as a potential way to save the company.

The new iteration of the company, Snow River Cooperative, exists because the dedicated workers received education and technical assistance from the UW

Center for Cooperatives. Ultimately, the owner financed 45 percent of the $1.1 million purchase price and two lenders who specialize in cooperatives, Shared Capital and the Local Enterprise Assistance Fund, provided the rest, along with a new line of credit.

Courtney told me that within a year of the purchase, divested of the former owner's significant financial draw, the new owners were able to give themselves a good raise, fully funded health care, and a dividend at the end of the year. "The worker co-op conversion has changed these peoples' lives," she said. "I don't know what they would have done if those jobs had gone away."

"There weren't a lot of other places to work." said Brian Sinclair, the plant's manager and now the co-op's general manager. Brian knew the Crandon plant had a unique product line and business opportunity, so he led the buyout and conversion effort with a group of fellow workers.

It's an inspiring story that shows what can happen when those who do the work get the help they need, take the reins, and share the rewards produced by the enterprise. Sometimes it's the employees who are the driving force rather than the founder.

I think Schumacher would have embraced the idea of the CommonWealth company as well. If we can make implementation of the Five Transitions more widespread, where might that lead? Maybe to businesses that embed a collection of attributes in their practice that take them beyond B Corp certification to becoming truly regenerative (rather than just less harmful) organizations. This is the CommonWealth company aspiration—to be actively engaged in implementing the Five Transitions in your own way, at your own pace, to whatever degree makes sense to you.

THE FIVE TRANSITIONS (A REMINDER)

- **Ownership:** from proprietary to widely shared and accessible to all
- **Leadership:** from original founder to next generation
- **Mission:** from unprotected to permanent preservation of purpose
- **Management and Governance:** from top-down control to participatory and democratic
- **Impact:** from business-as-usual to a certified B Corp force for good

ZINGERMAN'S

I think of Zingerman's Community of Businesses as a truly extraordinary company, one of the most forward-thinking and inspiring CommonWealth companies I know. And yet, after forty-three years, they have only completed three of the Five Transitions. They'll get to the rest, but these things take time (and sometimes there are other priorities).

In 1982, Ari Weinzweig and Paul Saginaw opened the Zingerman's doors in Ann Arbor. They wanted to make a place that served the good deli food they ate growing up in Detroit and Chicago, "a good corned beef sandwich and an organization with soul," said Paul.[13]

They made those things, and far more. They prospered and engaged their employees in unique ways. Ari and Paul developed more food-related businesses in the Ann Arbor area and committed to staying local and never franchising. When employees came to them with new ideas, they helped them form and finance companies under the Zingerman's name, and the Zingerman's Community of Businesses (ZCOB) evolved.

Along with the deli, ZCOB includes a bakehouse, a creamery, a coffee manufactory, Zingerman's Roadhouse restaurant, Miss Kim's Korean restaurant, a mail-order service, a food tours business, and a catering and events company. Another business, ZingTrain, is an influential leadership training and consulting institute. And there's Zingerman's Press, which publishes books and pamphlets about leadership, business practices, visioning, management, customer service, and a host of other topics. Many of them are written by Ari himself (see the Resources section).

Finally, there's ZingNet, which provides centralized core business services to all the other ZCOB businesses: human resources, marketing, information technology, finance, and accounting. The companies in this integrated business ecosystem are all located in the Ann Arbor area, and each business is represented on the governing Zingerman's Partners Group.

ZCOB business practices are highly sophisticated. Zingerman's has been a leading practitioner and proponent of open-book management (OBM). This management approach provides employees at all levels with access to the company's financial information and involves them in decision-making processes related to the business. The core idea is to foster a sense of ownership and responsibility among employees by making them aware of the financial health and performance of the company and, most importantly, what they can do to affect it.

Jack Stack, author of *The Great Game of Business*, is credited with pioneering OBM. Zingerman's drew inspiration from him and his work, and as they learned the method they began to teach it to other businesses through ZingTrain. South Mountain instituted OBM after several of us attended a ZingTrain session. It has become a hallmark of the South Mountain practice.

As ZCOB grew, Ari and Paul began to consider sharing the company's wealth with the employees and ensuring that ZCOB's values and mission would endure beyond their own tenure. In 2017, they offered ownership stakes to all employees. The new employee-owners receive annual dividends and the right to vote for Zingerman's Partners Group representation. In early 2023, Ari and Paul formally announced that they were "giving away the store" through the establishment of an unusual type of entity called a perpetual purpose trust (PPT). The "store" now consists of twelve Ann Arbor businesses, more than seven hundred employees, and $80 million in annual revenues.

Ari says, "While the phrase 'giving away the store' usually refers to poor negotiation skills, in our case it's a big win—the result of ten years of challenging conversations and complex work formally coming to fruition." The PPT ensures that Zingerman's mission and values will outlive the founders. Furthermore, the only beneficiary of this trust is Zingerman's *purpose*. Not a person, just the purpose. Zingerman's will stay Zingerman's. In perpetuity.

As for the Five Transitions and the B Corp, Ari says, "We're not much for certifications. We just naturally do it. Maybe we'll get certified someday."

Someday they probably will. But "just naturally doing it" can work, too. Regardless of whether or not they certify, they will continue to be an iconic CommonWealth company.

── PART TWO ──

EMPLOYEE OWNERSHIP DESIGNS

While the practices in chapter 2 are important aspects of mission-driven business, the foundation, in my view, is sharing ownership. Converting many employees to owners might transform the topography of tomorrow's small business landscape into a rich ecosystem of widespread empowerment and wealth-sharing.

"Ownership," says author Marjorie Kelly, "is the ultimate realm of economic power. We all belong there—in the same way that we all belong in the halls of democracy. It's time for us to own this place we call an economy. When more and more of us become comfortable entering the seemingly forbidden space of ownership—daring to dream together of remaking it—that's when we will truly own our future."[1]

In this part of the book, we will look at the intricacies of the different forms of employee ownership. Chapters 3 through 5 examine various aspects of the worker co-op and present it as the emblematic CommonWealth model. Chapter 6 explains why the employee stock ownership plan (ESOP) is tremendously important but only occasionally meets the Five Transitions standard. Chapter 7 examines the employee ownership trust (EOT), a newer corporate design that's on the rise in the United States. Chapter 8 considers some exciting recent employee ownership innovations and examines private equity's new interest.

One of these approaches may be right for you as you begin to navigate the Five Transitions to CommonWealth.

CHAPTER 3

THE WORKER CO-OP SOLUTION

W orker co-ops are businesses that are owned and democratically controlled by their employees. Each employee-owner has one share, and each share grants one voice and vote in the policies and direction of the company, and a share of the financial returns.

Having converted my former company to a worker co-op in 1987, and having been an advocate ever since, I admit to a bias—the worker co-op is the employee ownership structure I prefer. That may be because it's the one I know best. I have seen how remarkably well it can work at many scales. Although the worker co-op is an important employee ownership structure, it is not necessarily the right fit for all companies, and other models have great relevance as well.

This book covers the three major forms of employee ownership—worker co-ops, employee stock ownership plans (ESOPs), and employee ownership trusts (EOTs)—and several others that are more obscure, with the view that almost any form of employee ownership is better than none. But I lead with and devote the most attention to the worker co-op solution to mission-driven business succession. Conversion to a worker co-op is the most likely way to achieve some or all of the Five Transitions and become a CommonWealth company, because the principles are baked into the structure. Other forms of employee ownership can lead to precisely the same place, but their structures do not require it.

The relationship between leadership/management and company governance in a worker co-op is fundamentally different from business as usual. This structure creates an economic alternative to traditional corporate models, explicitly shares wealth, and goes a long way toward ensuring business continuity and a committed, engaged workforce—and I will show you how. But first, I want to give some context and general background about cooperatives.

COOPERATIVES WORLDWIDE

There are currently only about a thousand worker co-ops in the United States, but it is the largest form of employee ownership worldwide. The International Cooperatives Alliance (ICA), the global organization that represents and promotes cooperatives of all kinds (not just worker co-ops), estimates that there are roughly eighty-five thousand worker co-ops worldwide employing over 12 million people. They operate in every industry and at a variety of scales. For instance, the Mondragon Cooperatives in the Basque region of Spain has roughly eighty thousand employees.[1] The largest worker co-ops in the United States are the Drivers Cooperative, with more than eight thousand members,[2] and Cooperative Home Care Associates, with roughly two thousand.[3] Both are in New York.

The authors of *Cooperatives at Work* say that:

in places such as Emilia Romagna (Italy), The Basque Country (Spain), Quebec (Canada), South Korea, Argentina, Brazil, and India, high concentrations of worker co-ops have made significant and well-documented contributions to the health and well-being of individuals, families, and communities. Worker co-ops are thriving on every continent.[4]

Given the worldwide success of worker co-ops, they deserve more attention and wider adoption in the United States. This book aims to encourage that. However, worker cooperatives are only one type of cooperative. Their distinguishing characteristic is that the owners (often called members) are the workers employed by the company. Other common cooperative types are:

- consumer cooperatives (like food co-ops and REI), where shoppers are the members;
- producer cooperatives (like Organic Valley and Ocean Spray) that join forces for marketing or purchasing purposes;
- credit unions and cooperative banks, where those who use their services are the members;

- utility cooperatives, where ratepayers are the members;
- housing cooperatives, where residents are the members;
- multistakeholder cooperatives with multiple member types (like consumer-producer co-ops or consumer-worker co-ops); and
- cooperative holding companies and secondary cooperatives, where the members are other cooperatives.

The ICA uses seven principles to define cooperatives of all types:

- voluntary and open membership;
- democratic member control;
- member economic participation;
- autonomy and independence;
- provision of education, training, and information;
- cooperation among cooperatives; and
- concern for community.

Some in the cooperative world are advocating for an eighth principle involving diversity, equity, and inclusion.

Cooperatives are a significant economic force worldwide. The ICA says that "more than 12 percent of humanity is part of one of the three million cooperatives in the world."[5] John Restakis, in his book *Humanizing the Economy*, says:

The cooperative movement is by far the most durable and powerful grass-roots movement in the world. Cooperatives employ more people . . . than all the world's multinational companies combined. In its own quiet way, the cooperative vision continues to thrive and hold the keys to the emergence of an economic model that is capable of remaking and humanizing the current capitalist system.[6]

Cooperatives of all kinds are a major force even in the United States, although they largely fly under the economic radar. Familiar businesses like REI, Ace Hardware, Ocean Spray, and Organic Valley are cooperatives, but most people are unaware of this. There were over 4,760 credit unions in the United

States at the end of 2022, with 135 million people taking advantage of low-interest car loans and low mortgage rates.[7]

Since 1930, utility cooperatives have brought power to roughly 95 percent of US farms. Rural electric cooperatives have vast service territories; there are over 896 electric cooperatives that span forty-eight states and serve 42 million customers.[8] Most of these ratepayers are barely aware that they are cooperative members, and very few participate in governance—although they could.

John Restakis makes a compelling case for corollary values of cooperatives to society:

> Cooperatives replenish social capital in other ways as well. Members of cooperatives . . . are more likely to volunteer with other organizations. When they do, they bring the skills they acquired in their co-ops. Often, co-op staff and volunteers first learned their civic skills by setting up and running their co-ops. . . . If any social form were the ideal template for remaking society amid rampant individualism it is the cooperative.[9]

The worldwide impact of the many kinds of cooperatives provides context and backdrop for our more focused inquiry about worker cooperatives.

As the worker co-op becomes more widely known and understood, its inherent simplicity will be appealing to some business owners planning for succession. I think the model will gain further traction as Millennial and Gen Z entrepreneurs get wind of the concept, and as community development organizations and nonprofit developers build greater worker co-op infrastructure and expertise.

The worker co-op may also be an important strategy for avoiding business closures. Carolyn Edsell-Vetter of the Cooperative Development Fund of the Northeast told me:

> Boomers who failed to plan may find that their employees are their only alternative to liquidation and closure. We're already seeing emergency conversion attempts by concerned employees and community members trying to prevent businesses from shuttering. Community and economic developers, particularly in low-income, Black and brown neighborhoods, are already looking to co-ops as well.

THE WORKER CO-OP AND THE FIVE TRANSITIONS

Conversion to a worker co-op is the succession option that most often embodies the Five Transitions that this book advocates.

- **Ownership:** from proprietary to widely shared and accessible to all
- **Leadership:** from original founder to next generation
- **Mission:** from unprotected to permanent preservation of purpose
- **Management and Governance:** from top-down control to participatory and democratic
- **Impact:** from business-as-usual to a certified B Corp force for good

Other forms of employee ownership can also touch the bases of the Five Transitions; they just do so less often. We know this about ESOPs from extensive experience (chapter 6), but we have far less data about newer forms, like EOTs (chapter 7).

Cooperative businesses have the potential to bring wealth and rewards to those who have traditionally been excluded—the people who do the work. That's how it works in the four companies you've already encountered in this book: South Mountain, Snow River, Dean's Beans, and Zingerman's. It's equally true of the two companies that you'll meet later in this chapter: PixelSpoke and Ward Lumber.

WORKER CO-OP BENEFITS

Converting a business of any size to a worker co-op is good for the owners, the employees, the company, and the community in which the business operates. Compared to other business structures, worker co-ops create jobs with greater stability, are more equitable, and are more accountable. The benefits described here can also apply to other forms of employee ownership.

Good for Owners

If you own a small business, conversion to a worker co-op can have these benefits:

- If you are nearly ready to retire, it can facilitate a smooth exit and a reasonable return on your investment.

- In some circumstances, you can shelter your capital gains from taxation.
- If you are not close to retiring, you can finance the purchase and help build next-generation leadership to help ensure the company's success.
- Conversion to a worker co-op can preserve the business that took years to build and extend mission continuity by not selling to an outside entity that might dismantle or otherwise disrupt the business.
- Conversion to a worker co-op rewards employees for their role in helping you build your business.

Good for Employees

If you work in a small business, conversion to a worker co-op can benefit you in these ways:

- It provides the opportunity to share profits equitably based on hours of labor provided to the business.
- It extends the right to share in big-picture decision-making about issues that directly affect your work life.
- You can expect better job security and stability (employee-owners are less likely to get laid off, and worker cooperatives go belly-up less often than conventional businesses).
- There's great creative potential (to further shape the business you have already helped to build).

Good for the Business

A successful company may decide to convert to a worker co-op if it wants to attain these outcomes:

- Increase innovation and effectiveness through participatory collaborative management and development of an ownership culture.
- Attract, retain, and reward talented individuals by offering direct participation in governance and sharing financial surplus.
- Increase profitability and productivity—employees motivated by shared ownership care about and contribute to both.

- Increase resilience in tough times—worker co-ops tend to weather economic storms more successfully, as South Mountain did in 2008.
- Energize the workforce, because policies and initiatives get "buy-in" when they are collaboratively developed rather than dictated.

Good for the Community and the Economy

The community within which the business operates benefits in several ways:

- It is protected against the effects of outsourcing and market centralization, because worker co-ops tend to be rooted in place.
- Community wealth generated by the worker co-op circulates within the local economy and avoids wealth drain to distant investors.
- Local jobs are retained because companies owned by their employees are far less likely to leave the communities where their employee-owners live and are raising their families.
- Intergenerational wealth transfer opportunities are created for BIPOC (Black, Indigenous, People of Color) and Latinx workers, many of whom are small business employees.
- The worker co-op is an alternative to businesses closing their doors when founders are ready to retire (the largest single source of avoidable job loss in the United States).[10]

Good for Durability

Worker co-ops promote longevity, too. Most worker co-ops require an 80–90 percent vote of employee-owners if they want to sell the business. Some require 100 percent. Some add a requirement that a portion of the proceeds of a sale are donated to a charitable nonprofit to preclude potential personal financial gain from incentivizing a sale. Others are structured with an "indivisible reserve" that allocates a percentage of profits to a fund that can be used as operating capital but can never be distributed to individual members.

Some worker co-op bylaws have a "poison pill" to ensure that current employee-owners can't financially benefit from selling the company. Equal Exchange, the fair-trade coffee company, has a "never sell out" provision so that, in the event of a sale, proceeds are donated to another fair-trade company. Layering an ironclad perpetual purpose trust onto a worker co-op could give even greater protection, perhaps the most foolproof.

I encourage you to carefully examine these worker co-op benefits and consider how they might apply to your business.

PIXELSPOKE

All these benefits—for owners, workers, company, and community—are exemplified by PixelSpoke, a website design company in Oregon. Cameron Madill founded the company in 2003 with his dad, who was winding down a successful career as a tech executive. "We mostly had a blast working together, although there were some inevitable points of friction. I bought him out in 2009, and he remained as an employee until 2017," Cameron says. "But we were a business in search of a business model, doing the jack-of-all-trades thing. I was looking for a niche or focus that could make a stronger, more stable business model, but one with heart."

Becoming a Certified B Corp in 2014 was a hinge point for PixelSpoke because they had finally found their business philosophy peers—the heart part. But Cameron was seeking purpose, too. "At the time," says Cameron, "we had a few credit union clients. I realized that credit unions are incredible unsung heroes in the world of finance." In 2016, PixelSpoke homed in on credit unions as its primary clientele, and the purpose part of the business blossomed.

Cameron, then in his thirties, noticed that many in his industry—people in their fifties and sixties who owned agencies like his—seemed trapped by the businesses they had built. They had the prestige of owning and leading successful firms, and their companies supported a good lifestyle, "but to me, it felt like their work passion had left the building, and they were hanging on for lack of an alternative," he says. "I started thinking about myself and wondered, 'Do I want to be like that?'"

Cameron was concerned about overstaying, losing his commitment to the business he loved, and precluding other career possibilities. He wondered about the options in an intuitive, unhurried way. He thought about merging with a friendly agency. He thought about selling to a strategic buyer. Or could he try to sell to a few key internal people? None of these options resonated as a way to preserve "our purpose, culture, and values and the standard of service we deliver to our clients." He continued his search for a succession path, at a much younger age than most owners do.

At a B Corp Champions Retreat, a chance meeting with Blake Jones, one of the founders of Namaste Solar (and several other emblematic co-ops), introduced Cameron to the worker co-op. The concept clicked. During a process of discovery, he found each step to be a confirmation that led to a conclusion: "Yeah, this will have challenges like anything else, but it is clearly the right direction for us."

His colleagues were with him, and on January 1, 2020, they completed the eighteen-month process of transitioning from a single-member limited liability company (LLC) to a worker cooperative. An initial group of four employee-owners joined Cameron. People ask him why he would give up control of the company he spent seventeen years of his life building and that had only recently started delivering meaningful dividends beyond his salary. He attributes it to *living his beliefs* and cites five ways he was doing so:

- reducing inequality;
- increasing employee engagement;
- ensuring long-term sustainability;
- stimulating change to avoid stagnation; and
- sidestepping founder's syndrome.

The outcome: "The transition to a cooperative model allowed me to get a fair return for the company while gaining all those good things," Cameron says. "This conversion is one of the things in my life I'm most proud of. It was the birth of a brand-new company. It's a lot of hard work, but it accomplishes far more than a typical company sale."

At the end of 2023, Cameron stepped down as CEO and relinquished his ownership. He was replaced by a new president and a new CEO, both of whom had been with the company for some time. Currently, there are sixteen staff members, and eleven of them are now (in early 2024) owners, with several more about to join. An employment agreement defines Cameron's new role: coaching and strategic planning facilitation. He meets with the leaders for monthly sessions and leads quarterly strategic planning efforts with the entire team.

After the conversion, Kerala Taylor, one of the new owners, described what being an owner is like for her in an article titled "I Just Became a Co-Owner of My Company, and It's a Really Big Deal." She says:

I've signed the final papers and transferred my share to the company checking account. I'm now officially a co-owner. In practice, not much will change in my day-to-day work. I will still report to our CEO and my job responsibilities will remain the same.

It reminds me of buying my first home. When my husband and I moved in, it felt like any other move. We still had to contend with a jumble of poorly organized boxes, still had to find ways to fill blank walls, still had to write a painful check at the beginning of each month.

But I've come to understand that renting and owning are worlds apart. As homeowners, we're more invested in our community and go to greater lengths to meet our neighbors. We work on improvements. We take pride in our home because it's ours. It's much more than a comfortable place to put our feet up at the end of the day. In my previous jobs, it was like renting. I was there to work, not to build. Now I'm here to build.[11]

This commonly happens when companies become worker co-ops. Ownership is a powerful change, or as Kerala says, "a really big deal."

As for Cameron, he's gradually assembling a new future and his story provides essential lessons for business founders: don't be stymied by convention, plan for succession, and make sure your timing is right.

After converting South Mountain Company to a co-op, it took me 35 years to fully relinquish ownership and employment and pass the reins to new leadership. Maybe I was too slow; it only took Cameron four! What's right for me may not be right for you. Beat the bushes and find the right path for you.

BUSINESS OWNERSHIP SOLUTIONS

Rob Brown is one of the people responsible for expanding the number of worker co-ops. He is the director of the Business Ownership Solutions division of the Cooperative Development Institute (CDI), a nonprofit whose mission is to build a cooperative economy in the northeastern United States. Rob and his small staff consistently help existing businesses transition from sole ownership or partnerships to worker cooperatives. As of this writing, CDI has led thirty-three businesses through transitions to worker co-ops, creating ownership opportunities for more than 570 employees and helping them secure over $34 million in capital to buy those businesses. Rob says:

> For many businesses, employee ownership may be the most viable exit plan. The workers whose jobs are at stake are the most motivated to "keep the lights on." This strategy could save businesses and jobs and offer workers the opportunity to improve incomes and build wealth through ownership, all while deepening local ownership and control of businesses and making our economy more equitable and resilient.[12]

Rob and his colleagues assemble teams of accountants, attorneys, and financers for each conversion and coordinate all the particulars of the transaction. They educate owners and employees in the skills of ownership and participatory democratic management both before and after the transaction. This is an essential aspect of their services. The goal is not just to complete new worker co-op conversions; it's to create successful, impactful, and enduring companies.

One of their conversions was Ward Lumber, which is a shining example of the potential for worker co-op conversions to influence the direction of businesses during the silver tsunami.

WARD LUMBER

The Ward Lumber Company straddles a two-lane road in the small rural Adirondack town of Jay, New York. Behind the hardware store and lumber yard is the Ward Pine Mill, one of the largest producers of white pine lumber in the state. Sixty miles away, in another small town called Malone, is Ward Lumber's second store and yard.

The company's origins go back to 1890 (another hundred-year company, like Snow River and King Arthur), when Harvey Ward used logs supplied by local farmers and landowners to mill the lumber that farmers needed for building. His four sons ran the business as Ward Brothers, and in 1944 one of them,

Sidney Sr., became the owner. He began a retail lumber organization and also accumulated, over time, more than five thousand acres of timberland.

When Sidney Sr. passed in 1970, his son, Sidney Jr., became the third-generation owner. In 1997, he and his wife Janet sold the business to their sons, who became the fourth-generation owners. Sidney III, "Jay," was now president, and his brother Jeff was senior vice president of manufacturing.

Jay Ward started working in the family business when he was eight, stacking hardwood stickers (the wood pieces that separate rows of drying lumber) for fifty cents an hour. He kept working summers as he grew up, finished high school, and went to Utica College. Originally, he had no intention of returning to the family business. But while home for his mom's fiftieth birthday, he looked up at Jay Mountain and thought, "Why don't I live here?" Then he gave his mom her birthday present: "I'm moving home."

That was in July 1988. On August 1, he went to work. He had no office and had to create his own role. His dad was old-school—kept it all in his head, didn't easily delegate responsibility, and made others prove themselves, including his kids. Jay says there was always a line outside his dad's door with people waiting for decisions from the guy who had his finger on the pulse of every nook and cranny of the business. When Jay became president in 1997 after the purchase from his parents, he knew he didn't want a line outside his door all day. He wanted to find a different way to manage and to empower employees to make their own decisions.

Worker Co-op Transition

As Jay approached retirement age and found that his daughters were not interested in running the business, he decided to honor the employees who had helped him build the company by converting to a worker co-operative. In 2018, he broached the idea with the employees at the annual company financial review. They didn't really know what to think. To some, it seemed like a crazy idea.

Shortly thereafter, Jay met Rob Brown at the Vermont Employee Ownership Center's annual conference and hired him to help determine if the conversion made sense. A transition steering committee was established with six people drawn from both stores and several long-term support staff as advisers.

A lengthy process concluded in 2021 when the employees formed the Ward Lumber Worker Cooperative and purchased the company from Jay. Most of the sixty employees—forty-eight at last count and rising—are now also owners; they share equally in the business, each with one voting share on policy matters.

The purchase price for the business with annual revenues of $18 million was $3.6 million. Roughly half of this sum was financed by Jay with a thirty-year low-interest note. The other half came from a $1.55 million loan from the Cooperative Fund of the Northeast (CFNE), a lending nonprofit, and a $250,000 grant from Empire State Development, a New York State economic development agency. The New York Small Business Development Center (NYSBDC) helped Ward access the grant funds. This was the first time such grant funds were used for a worker co-op conversion in the state, and Ward is the first worker co-op in New York's North Country.

Although the amount of the state grant was a small part of the overall purchase price, it was a tipping point in gathering employee support and resolve. Angela Smith, formerly of NYSBDC, who wrote the grant application with Rob Brown, told me, "Ward Lumber is the only sizable business in its area. It provides good jobs with good benefits and is very important to its community."

Paying a Visit

I spent two splendid October days at Ward, walking the grounds, driving around with Jay, talking to many of the employees, meeting with the top CEO candidate to replace Jay (who was in town for interviews), and meeting with the board of directors.

Except for the yard and mill site—covered with buildings, equipment, and inventory—there's nothing around, just mountains as far as you can see. One of the yard workers said, "It's great working outside here, 'cause if you get stressed, you can just take a deep breath, look up at Jay Mountain, and in a heartbeat you're all settled down."

Along with being fully stocked with hardware and tools, the store has snacks, drinkware, and other items not usually found in a lumber yard. There's even a shed with animal feed for goats, chickens, alpacas, and cows. And next to the front door, there was a big rack of pumpkins. It's a place of constant movement, like a choreographed dance: trucks and people in and out; forklifts circling; swarms of people working, talking, and joking. Chief jokester seemed to be Roger, who was everywhere and whose shirt label said under his name, "Essential Since 2019." (After the federal government deemed Ward an "essential business" during the COVID-19 pandemic and allowed it to remain open, Jay decided to label everyone's work clothes with "Essential Since" their date of hire.) The place oozes unaffected team spirit and feels like a genuinely happy place, and when you talk to people privately, the message is the same.

The Co-op in Practice

Employees are eligible for ownership after working for six months and completing a variety of ownership preparation tasks. They pay a nominal $1,000 for a share. Member dividends are distributed at the end of each profitable year based on the number of hours worked. The conversion coincided with years of growth and high profits. In the first year, the average dividend was $34,000; in the second, it was $22,000. This is on top of good wages and excellent benefits. Operations manager C. J. Young told me, "For me, the first-year patronage dividend was life-changing—it helped me buy a house. With that done, I'll start putting it all into a retirement account, something not all Americans have."

These are unusually high annual patronage dividends for a worker co-op. It's one thing to share the wealth when there's not much wealth to share—it's another thing when there is, like at Ward.

The current board of directors is made up of seven seasoned and dedicated employees, elected by the forty-eight owners. Some are managers; some are non-managers. More people run for these volunteer seats than the number of positions available. With the help of outside advisers like CDI, the board and its committees are deeply engaged in the long-term process of learning to be a co-op and building a successful ownership culture. Jay stayed on to help with the hiring and onboarding of a new CEO and then retired from that position at the end of 2023. He has remained at Ward to manage purchasing, his great love.

I asked board members what caused them to run and commit so much time. Debby Straight, the chief financial officer who was hired by Jay's mother and has been there for forty years, said, "I've been here forever. I'm committed to this company and already felt a sense of ownership. I wanted to be part of this great step forward."

The board vice president, Scott Christian, said, "My dad once told me, 'If you want to succeed as a leader, look to the person sitting to your right and the person sitting to your left. If you help them succeed, you will succeed.' That's the kind of leader I aspire to be—the kind that helps others succeed. As a board member, I can do that."

Bedrock

Jay observes that "in all companies, there's going to be transition, either by design or default." Why not by design? The many positive lessons of the Ward Lumber succession experience are inspiring.

One that is less positive but important to note is that Jay Ward built a tremendous team, but he failed to train an internal replacement for his job as CEO. He did train a replacement for the other most important job in the company—managing purchasing—but after a year, it was clear that was not going to work out. Now they will begin to build a bench for all management jobs in anticipation of the next management and leadership transition, which is bound to come much sooner than the last one, which took thirty-one years.

What would have happened if Jay had not stumbled on the worker-co-op idea? It's hard to say, but Jay was committed to not selling to a private equity buyer. He thinks it's important that small businesses stay local and don't become prey to private equity sharks, as he's seen happen to other companies in the purchasing co-op Ward is a part of.

Ward Lumber is a bedrock small-town company that provides honest work and good livelihoods to members of local communities. They provide an important essential service for the area they serve. They are the epitome of the B Corp goal of making business be a force for good. And now they are a worker co-op.

As one of the new owners said: "We're a family business creating a new family."

CHAPTER 4

WORKER CO-OP RESOURCES

C onversion to a worker co-op is not uncomplicated, but there are knowledgeable and experienced guides eager to support the journey. They include cooperative developers, valuators, accountants, attorneys, and financers.

When we converted South Mountain Company to a worker co-op in 1987, the infrastructure to support such organizations barely existed, and there were only a few worker co-ops to use as models. Most early US worker co-ops still exist after forty to fifty years: Red Sun Press (1974), Fedco Seeds (1978), the Union Cab Cooperative (1979), Alvarado Street Bakery (1979), Cooperative Home Care Associates (1986), and Equal Exchange (1986). Many have expanded significantly.

We were lucky to find the Industrial Cooperatives Association (now called the ICA Group) and their attorney, Peter Pitegoff, to help us. Founded in 1977, ICA Group is the oldest nonprofit in the United States doing worker co-op development. Allison Curtis, ICA's business conversions program director, tells me that they have been involved in roughly sixty worker co-op conversions.

ICA has grown. Ten years ago, when David Hammer became executive director, he was one of three people at ICA. Another served at their spin-off, LEAF (Local Enterprise Assistance Fund), which was started in 1982 to provide financing for cooperatives, and the third, a bookkeeper, served both organizations. Today, ICA has sixteen employees, LEAF has seventeen, and Hammer thinks it is likely that they will grow significantly in the coming years.

Hammer told me, "For many years, the history of worker cooperatives in the United States was pretty much the history of the ICA Group."

WORKER CO-OP INFRASTRUCTURE

That is hardly the case today. A collection of organizations now exists, grows, collaborates with one another, and makes the worker cooperative movement expand. Cooperative economy researcher Danny Spitzberg at the University of California said in an email in February 2024:

> Ownership is having a moment. Since 2022, a dozen new ownership consultancies appeared, and several software start-ups raised funding to "productize" the conversion process. This cottage industry is transforming shared ownership from an economic possibility into a market of established or newly branded models, opening the door to capital that has historically been at odds with new models.

Project Equity

Hilary Abell is the cofounder of Project Equity in Oakland, California. It is one of three organizations—along with the Cooperative Development Institute (CDI) Business Ownership Solutions division (introduced in chapter 3) and ICA—currently responsible for most US worker co-op conversions. Project Equity has been involved in more than a hundred conversions.

Hilary was bitten by the co-op bug in the 1990s when she was one of the first ten employee-owners at Equal Exchange, the influential fair-trade coffee worker co-op in Massachusetts that has more than one hundred employee owners. Before founding Project Equity with Alison Lingane in 2014, Hilary was executive director of an organization called WAGES (now called Prospera) that focuses exclusively on developing and launching cooperative businesses owned by Latina immigrant women. She says that in the early WAGES days, she led a "small but mighty team" that had very close relationships with the women in the co-ops because WAGES provided ongoing technical assistance.

"I was inspired to see them gaining confidence, skills, having health insurance for the first time, and earning far more than previously," Hilary told me.

"We performed data-driven program evaluation. The first time we examined their tax returns, we found that their family incomes had risen an average of 40 percent since they became employee-owners." The last time they measured family incomes during her tenure, a half dozen years later, the increase was up to 80 percent!

"Oh my god," she says, "it was totally life-changing for workers who have so many barriers to economic security. Those successes drove me and my colleagues at Project Equity to want to scale and grow the numbers of worker co-ops." Not only are they doing more and more conversions, but they are working with larger and larger companies.

Hilary recently left Project Equity and joined the US Department of Labor as chief of the new employee ownership division. This is an exciting development that indicates the credibility that employee ownership is gaining. Project Equity continues to thrive and has expanded its services to include employee ownership trust conversions.

W2O, DAWI, and USFWC

Project Equity, ICA, CDI, and similar organizations, along with some that provide conversion financing, are members of Workers to Owners (W2O), a collaborative of worker co-op organizations that share information, data, and methodologies with each other.

W2O is a program of the Democracy at Work Institute (DAWI), one of two national organizations that support the US worker co-op movement. DAWI provides education and research to the public and develops resources to encourage the growth of the worker co-op movement. DAWI's sister organization is the US Federation of Worker Cooperatives (USFWC). The USFWC is a grassroots membership organization that advocates for and provides benefits to its member worker cooperatives.

I apologize for loading you up with organizational names and acronyms, but they're all important parts of the expanding employee ownership landscape.

Along with the two national organizations, additional worker cooperative development infrastructure and capital providers have mushroomed in recent years, as Spitzberg said. Some of them are quite different from the organizations described so far. Like Start.coop.

Start.coop

Howard Brodsky cofounded CCA Global Partners in 1984. It became one of the largest privately held companies in the United States with aggregate revenues of over $10 billion at the time of his retirement. But it wasn't like any other business; it was comprised of fourteen cooperatives of different types, serving a million family businesses.

The apple doesn't fall far from the tree. In 2004, Howard's son Greg founded and led a division of CCA called the Bike Cooperative, a purchasing co-op of three hundred independent bike retailers. Then he formed another purchasing co-op, for the craft brewing industry. "In our family," Greg says, "we were talking cooperatives when other families were talking sports."

Greg served on the board of CDI for ten years and as board chair for three of those. He loved the work that CDI does with worker co-ops and housing co-ops, but he was frustrated by the slow pace of US cooperative development. He and his dad saw an opportunity to expedite growth by building systems to scale co-op development. They were imagining how to "break open the black box" by making the process less mysterious and by removing cumbersome friction points for entrepreneurs. Having worked in a tech start-up for a few years, Greg wondered if he could combine the best of cooperative values and lean start-up methodology in a new organization.

Start.coop was born.

Today, the organization is a Boston-based accelerator program experiencing tremendous success working with early-stage entrepreneurs seeking scale and social impact using shared ownership models. In five years, they have launched forty-five co-ops, including the nine-thousand-member Drivers Cooperative, a platform cooperative built around a mobile app that is owned and used by its members. According to Greg, the drivers/owners earn 30 percent more than Lyft and Uber drivers.

All co-ops formed by Start.coop are currently start-ups, but they expect to begin using their method for conversions as well, and they are talking to Project Equity and ICA Group about partnering with them.

"We believe that if you care deeply about wealth inequality, then co-ops should be your preferred ownership model," says Greg. "But people don't always understand what it means to be cooperatively owned, so we're focused on helping co-ops scale and updating the narrative. Co-ops level the playing field, especially for economically disadvantaged groups—women, minorities, immigrants, family business owners, and veterans. By investing in co-op start-ups, helping them become stronger businesses, and demonstrating their ability to scale, we have the potential to start reversing wealth inequality for the next generation."

A worthy goal and, in its brief history, Start.coop has already made significant impact.

State Statutes

Every state in the United States has at least one cooperative statute. Some of them go back to the late 1800s and were originally drafted for agriculture cooperatives. In many cases, they have been modernized, expanded, and become more flexible.

Many states now have specific *worker* cooperative statutes that provide legal frameworks for the establishment, operation, and governance of worker cooperatives. One of the strongest was enacted in Massachusetts in 1982. South Mountain was able to organize as a worker cooperative under this statute when it converted in 1987. Meegan Moriarty, a legal analyst at the US Department of Agriculture who specializes in cooperative statutes, told me in a conversation that the Massachusetts statute has been used as a model by many other states. Worker cooperative statutes continue to be enacted; according to Meegan, approximately twenty states have them today.

Legal Support for Co-ops

If the worker cooperative is ever to play a significant role in the American economy, Jason Wiener is sure to be part of the reason. "I feel like I was one of the very last progenies of the American dream when public school teachers like my parents could afford a home and vacations," he told me. "My youth sowed the seeds of my ideology about middle-out economics [which identifies the buying power of the middle class as the necessary ingredient for job creation and economic growth]. I became an attorney, and middle-out became my North Star to understand how transactional law and a humane and people-centered version of that could be a calling to help build a new economic structure."

By 2009, Wiener felt it was time to get on with it, so he left big law and New York City and headed west to Boulder, Colorado. He became general counsel for Namaste Solar during its worker co-op conversion. They have become one of the largest and most influential US worker co-ops.

Six years later, he hung out a shingle and his law firm has been spearheading the cooperative movement ever since. "I realized the legal side of it was one sliver," he said, "but it was the broader packaging of economic modeling, organizational development, and organizational psychology that was an essential part of the puzzle. So, we became what I consider to be a legal design-build firm, and we took that cargo on the road."

Along with worker co-ops, Jason's firm has represented electric co-ops, credit unions, housing co-ops, consumer co-ops, and producer co-ops. The bulk of the practice is devoted to broad-based alternative ownership models. Many, if not most, of its thirty to forty-five client companies are B Corps or benefit corporations (Jason Wiener | p.c. is both), and many are already cooperatives. In the world of cooperatives, this growing ten-person firm is a significant force, nationwide.

Jason's bottom-line operational philosophy is that the legal structure of the co-op cannot be counted on to succeed without significant accompanying organizational and cultural development work. That notion aligns with my longtime personal sense that we need to encourage early ownership conversions with long runways to leadership transitions. I'll explain what I mean with the story of Trillium Architects.

TRILLIUM ARCHITECTS COOPERATIVE

Elizabeth DiSalvo spent nineteen years building Trillium Architects into an important Connecticut firm. Trillium specializes in high-performance residential work and is consistently busy and profitable. At age 57, Elizabeth decided she wanted to convert her firm to a worker co-op, work for another ten years, and build a leadership team to succeed her during that time. Her dedicated group of employees appeared to be ready to engage.

She asked my small new consulting firm, Abrams+Angell, to help her. We formed a steering committee consisting of Elizabeth and four of the company's twelve employees. We enlisted an accountant and an attorney well-versed in co-ops and began making the key decisions and building a value proposition.

Elizabeth had no idea what the company was worth, but she had a sense of what she hoped to gain to provide for her personal long-term financial security. It turned out, in this case, that the accountants' valuation and Elizabeth's needs were in sync. Elizabeth agreed to a $1 million sale price to be paid as a ten-year note at 5 percent interest. The entire amount will be paid to her from company profits in annual principal and interest installments.

A ten-year earnings projection by accountants at Whittlesey (who also did the original company valuation) showed that the company should easily be able to fulfill that commitment, and a provision in the purchase agreement provides that Elizabeth will accept delayed payments in the event that one or more bad years make it tough for the company to pay. She also agreed to an employment contract that specifies she will continue in her role as CEO (her title is actually CVO—chief vision officer) for that ten-year period and stipulates her salary (with bonuses if company performance exceeds predictions).

The steering committee decided that the buy-in fee would be $12,500 and all employees who served for two years would be eligible to become owners. As we worked through the various decisions and document creation, and as the group became convinced that this was truly going to happen, they became more and more involved in understanding the finances, the responsibilities, the risks, the potential rewards, and the intense learning that would be necessary to succeed. They crafted a mission statement, guiding principles, and a decision-making matrix. Attorney PJ Deluhery, who has worked on scores of worker co-op conversions, prepared the transaction documents.

Each employee can purchase an ownership share of a thriving architectural practice for a relatively modest investment (which goes into their internal capital account and will be refunded when they leave the company). Not only do they get the company, but they get Elizabeth, too (for ten years) to help ensure company success and reduce risk to the new owners.

Elizabeth gets a winning trifecta: the financial security she hoped for, a new level of commitment from the colleagues she has nurtured, and the joy of taking the company she loves to a new place as she approaches retirement. On January 1, 2024, after eleven months of planning, Trillium Architects LLC became Trillium Architects Cooperative, Inc. All five steering committee members who had worked diligently to address the issues took the plunge. More new owners are soon to come.

At Trillium, all the stars aligned. Willing seller, willing buyers. A well-run profitable company where people enjoy their work. A founding owner with a collaborative bent whose mid-career transition would provide ample time for building new leadership capacity, relieving the pressure that often accompanies co-op conversions undertaken when the founder is ready to retire. Most companies don't think about succession when the founder is in the prime of her career. But they should, and more are coming to understand this. The benefits can be tremendous.

But how do you finance a co-op conversion when the stars are not as aligned as they were at Trillium?

FINANCING CO-OP CONVERSIONS

After co-founding a boutique consulting firm that "specialized in arcane areas of banking," Andy Danforth found that he wanted to do something with more meaning.

He joined the board of the Cooperative Fund of the Northeast (CFNE), a socially responsible lending organization that has helped to finance many worker co-ops. He began to specialize in financing for worker co-op conversions and housing co-op development. He has been involved in assembling financing for more than fifty worker co-ops and has vast experience in how these transactions work.

"Nearly 100 percent of co-op conversions have some level of owner financing," says Andy, "usually 50 percent or more of the total buyout cost." Others in the world of co-op finance that I have spoken with agree with this assessment. Courtney Berner, the executive director of the University of Wisconsin Center for Cooperatives, tells me that all the conversions they have done, except one, have been 100 percent owner financed. The exception was Snow River, which you read about in chapter 2.

The rest comes from mission-driven lenders like CFNE, which has grown, during Andy's time on the board, from a $2 million organization to a $50 million organization. Most of CFNE's funds come from impact investors who receive a small return.

Carolyn Edsell-Vetter came to CFNE after nineteen years with A Yard and A Half Landscaping, in the Boston suburbs, where she led their conversion to a worker co-op and served as co-CEO from 2014 to 2019. She is the CFNE program director who works with applicants and borrowers to assess feasibility. She notes that CFNE "rarely says no to applicants; more often, we say 'not yet,' and then we provide technical assistance to help businesses get to the point where they can successfully borrow to finance conversion."

Financing a worker co-op conversion is fundamentally different from financing a conventional business sale, where the provision of capital generally comes hand-in-hand with a share of control of the business and the potential to maximize profits from the investment. Worker cooperatives, by definition, put control in the hands of workers, and they distribute earnings primarily based on the value and quantity of the workers' labor.

In addition to loans from economic development nonprofits like CFNE, sometimes there are loans from community banks and credit unions, direct public offerings, assistance grants from public agencies, and philanthropic capital. Equal Exchange has recently used crowdfunding to finance expansion, which is now permissible due to a new federal regulation. The new owner buy-in fees are not used to finance the purchase. They are the new owners' "skin in the game" and go into each member's individual capital account.

CFNE has financed more than thirty-five conversions since 2012. In many cases, they also provide for worker co-ops' ongoing capital needs. Carolyn is seeing increasing demand and larger and larger co-op conversions; for these, CFNE often partners with other co-op-friendly loan funds.

CFNE is one of a collection of growing organizations providing financing for worker co-ops. Some others are Capital Impact Partners, Common Wealth Revolving Loan Fund, the Shared Capital Fund, the National Cooperative Bank, LEAF, Greg Brodsky's Equitable Economy Fund, and Blake Jones's Kachuwa Impact Fund.

Carolyn says that, from her vantage point, there is sufficient capital currently available for co-op conversion financing. But as the size and number of worker co-op increases, there will be a growing need for new sources. We are at a tipping point, she notes, and the tide is turning. She also points out that if we are serious about transferring assets from BIPOC (Black, Indigenous, People of Color) business owners to BIPOC employees, we will need more mission-aligned funders because "Black and Latinx business owners may have less ability to provide long-term notes because of the racial differences in US intergenerational wealth transfer."

There's also a need for the federal government to level the financing playing field. In a 2024 article examining whether employee ownership is ready for a wave of business owner retirements, the authors write:

> The leading source of small business financing nationally is federally guaranteed loans through the US Small Business Administration. The employee ownership field, of course, knows this. Six years ago, Congress passed the Main Street Employee Ownership Act, which was supposed to make these loans available to employee-owned businesses. But there have been numerous bureaucratic obstacles—these center on a requirement for a "personal guarantee." When a single family owns the business, they often provide the personal guarantee, which typically pledges their home as collateral. But if you have multiple owners, whose home is put at risk?[1]

Current advocacy is attempting to change this requirement. The federal small business support system is large, but, to date, it has not been widely used to support conversion to employee ownership. Modest policy interventions could change this and broaden the capital available to fund worker co-op conversions.

BARRIERS TO WORKER CO-OP ADOPTION

The Sustainable Economies and Law Center, which has written the most comprehensive legal guide to worker cooperatives that I have found, says this about worker cooperatives:

> Given the advantages of worker cooperatives compared with investor-owned and other employee-owned forms of business, the relative rarity of worker co-ops [in the United States] is surprising and is often attributed to workers' lack of capital and expertise. But in light of the rapidly changing nature of the economy, the growing interest in worker cooperatives,

the constant growth of employee ownership, and the structural advantages presented by worker cooperatives, the worker cooperative sector is only likely to expand in coming years. Given this trend, business and legal professionals should become familiar with the cooperative structure and legal rules that govern cooperative enterprises.[2]

Although there is a steady tailwind filling the worker co-op sails, there are headwinds as well. There are more complex barriers to widespread adoption than the need for additional capital, such as the lack of familiarity, unfounded fears, and misperceptions.

Let's start with familiarity. Greg Brodsky of Start.coop says, "Most people have heard the word cooperative, but only 11 percent can accurately define one. Most entrepreneurs aren't familiar with cooperatives and don't know that they are a viable business model." Very few founders, employees, business advisers, financial planners, accountants, and attorneys know about the worker co-op option.

Then there's the fear factor. I asked Dave Hammer at ICA if one of the reasons that co-ops are not more widespread is a general fear of democracy. His reply: "Absolutely—a fear of democracy or just a fear of losing control. You went through this process at South Mountain, you know that changing the governance and management structure are significant changes that require time and education. Founders may be concerned that the employees don't have the ability to run the company. But with the proper training they can, and that can make the company much stronger."

That's my experience. In spades.

The concerns expressed by Greg and Dave—a lack of familiarity and the fear of democracy and loss of control—are fundamental and essential. But I think there are two other very important issues.

Leadership Misconceptions

The first is a misunderstanding about leadership that needs correction. Successful worker co-ops, like all other successful organizations, need effective leadership. Leaderless organizations of all kinds have historically tended to have short lives (Alcoholics Anonymous is a notable exception).

Nobody I know who advocates for and understands worker cooperatives downplays the importance of effective leadership. Worker co-ops do not lack leadership. Rather, they distinguish management leadership from governance leadership, with governance being controlled by the employee-owners. This is a critical distinction that needs to be understood.

Every successful worker co-op has a CEO or a general manager and a leadership team. These managers oversee operations and run the company day-to-day. As for governance, the employees who comprise the elected board of directors make decisions about company policy and direction, not operations. At South Mountain, we didn't want people drawing straws for who makes the stairway; we wanted, of course, the best stair builder to oversee that complex task. And just like the stair builder was trained in that craft, the co-op must make an intentional investment in governance training to ensure that worker-owners are well equipped to make governance decisions.

The key here is learning to lead without relying solely on hierarchies of power. Hierarchies of expertise, on the other hand, are embraced.

The Worker Co-op Brand

The second misperception is a branding problem. Greg Brodsky says, "The term *worker co-op* has come to have a hippie-dippie ring to it. Maybe it's misnamed. Maybe it needs to be called something different."

I don't think so. The worker cooperative has such a long and storied history worldwide that I don't think we should change the name. We need instead to change the perception and the connotation and provide good examples that debunk the misconceptions. There's nothing hippie-dippie about Ward Lumber or Snow River. Far from it.

As founders considering start-up or succession learn more about these important aspects of leadership and the nature of business democracy, the fears may subside. As the benefits and history of worker co-ops become more well known, that name may be celebrated and become an advantage. But the hesitations of those whose life-experience may differ from ours must be taken seriously, and it is our challenge to address their concerns. Now that there is a maturing worker co-op infrastructure that can provide the information as well as the practical skills to demystify the conversion process, the table may be set for the growth of the worker co-op option.

In *The Alternative*, author Nick Romeo says:

> Worker-owned cooperatives are often dismissed as an idealistic but inefficient business model, the sort of thing that might work for an upscale grocery store or boutique bakery in a progressive town, but not a serious alternative to the standard corporation. At a 2019 conference, the economist Larry Summers characterized worker-owned cooperatives as sleepy and short-sighted. "When you put workers in charge of firms and you give them substantial control over the firms," he said, "the one thing you do not get is expansion. You get more for the people who are already there."[3]

Romeo continues, "Mondragon demolishes this stereotype." He is referring to the Mondragon Cooperatives in the Basque region of Spain, which you will read about in chapter 5.

CHAPTER 5

WORKER CO-OP ECOSYSTEMS

To have big impact, you don't necessarily have to build big businesses. This chapter is about the influence that can be achieved by cooperation among cooperatives and the propagation that can result from proximity. Businesses come together in different ways to amplify their impact: through secondary cooperatives of similar peer businesses; cooperative ecosystems with diverse actors, niches, and interdependencies; and place-based cooperative networks.

The most enduring, sizable, influential, and successful ecosystem examples in the world are the Mondragon Cooperatives in the Basque region of Spain and the vast network of cooperatives in the Emilia-Romagna province in Northern Italy. I'll tell a little about both before bringing it home to US endeavors.

The research and interviews for this chapter inspired me so much that I believe the cooperative ecosystem subject could make a compelling book of its own. I hope this brief exposure whets your appetite.

MONDRAGON

In 1941, a young priest named Jose Maria Arizmendiarrieta was assigned by the Catholic Church to the Basque town of Mondragon. When he arrived, the area was locked in poverty and still recovering from the devastation of the Spanish Civil War. He believed that part of his service should be to raise the economic fortunes of the people of Mondragon.

He founded a technical school. In 1955, five graduates established a small worker co-op to manufacture kerosene stoves. More cooperative businesses formed during the rest of the 1950s. Arizmendiarrieta encouraged the 1959 formation of a cooperative credit union to finance more co-ops.

Arizmendiarrieta died in 1976, but the Mondragon Corporacion Cooperativa (MCC), which binds together all the cooperative enterprises that began on his watch, continued to grow and thrive. A research institute was established to help with technology development, and in the 1990s, Mondragon University, a private university dedicated primarily to the study of business and commerce, opened its doors.

Today, MCC is an association of more than 250 cooperative businesses, in addition to the bank, the research institute, and the university. Of the eighty thousand employees, roughly 75 percent are owners. Each co-op's highest-paid executive makes at most six times the salary of its lowest-paid employee. There are no outside shareholders; instead, after a temporary contract, new workers who have proved themselves may become member-owners of their co-ops. MCC's gross revenues in 2021 were over 11 billion euros, making it the largest corporation in the Basque region and one of the largest in Spain.

The co-ops include Spain's largest producer of home appliances, leading tool and die makers, and other industrial companies that make forklifts, wind turbine parts, bicycles, automotive components, nails, wire, boilers, health and exercise equipment, furniture, woodworking and machine tools, specialized electronic products, manufacturing machinery and robots, and dozens of other products. MCC's Eroski is the largest supermarket chain in Spain; it engages in catering, dairy farming, greenhouse horticulture, and rabbit breeding as well. Other co-ops provide engineering, market research, banking, insurance, pensions, consulting, and a host of other services. Mondragon has created a total system wherein one can learn, work, shop, and live within a cooperative environment.

Success is an institution at Mondragon. There are several new start-ups each year, and very few have failed. According to the US Small Business Administration, more than 50 percent of US business start-ups fail within the first five years.[1]

But there are questions. What drives MCC's recent interest in export and locating new plants overseas? Can it continue dancing on the tightrope between ongoing success in a global business climate and holding true to its core values? Why doesn't its environmental consciousness (which seems higher than normal but not extraordinary) match the concern about social equity and economic democracy?

During a visit to Mondragon long ago, I asked those questions. The answers were pragmatic: MCC's primary purpose is the creation of safe, secure lifelong jobs and prosperity for the employee-owners. Sometimes, compromise is needed to achieve these goals. I remember someone reciting the informal Mondragon motto: "This is not heaven, and we are not angels."

For example, the original ratio of top-to-bottom pay was 3:1. As the co-ops grew, it was hard to attract top management talent within that pay scale. They changed the limit to 6:1, and today it averages 5:1. Mondragon's top-to-bottom pay ratio remains extraordinarily low compared to the average ratio of US Standard & Poor's (S&P) 500 firms, which, in 2022, was 272:1.[2] As Nick Romeo says in *The Alternative*, "The notion that astronomically high CEO compensation is necessary for business efficacy is a myth: a potent alternative model already exists at scale and needs only to be implemented more widely."[3]

Mondragon Cooperatives continues to balance democratic social goals with survival in competitive markets. It is passionately committed to cooperative principles and always trying to extend democratic values to traditional enterprises that it acquires.

I could write a full chapter about Mondragon, but the story has been told well and in detail by others. One early account is Roy Morrison's book with the great title *We Build the Road as We Travel*. Two of the best and most recent are the Mondragon chapter in Nick Romeo's book *The Alternative* and the dense and illuminating collection of essays edited by Christina Clamp and Michael Peck called *Humanity @ Work & Life*.

Mondragon has had tremendous worldwide influence. Why wouldn't it? A network of worker cooperatives has, in the last seventy years, transformed a poverty-stricken area into a thriving region full of opportunity. There's at least one other area where that has happened in a significant way.

EMILIA-ROMAGNA

The Emilia-Romagna region of Northern Italy, the province anchored by the beautiful and vibrant city of Bologna, has a population of 4.5 million, virtually full employment, and a high level of prosperity that is 28 percent higher than the

European Union average.[4] At the core of this strikingly successful economy are thousands of worker cooperatives that have a strong collaborative relationship with the regional government. In *Humanizing the Economy*, John Restakis writes:

> The intensity of the region's entrepreneurial activity is staggering. . . . At the foundation of this economic powerhouse and a key reason for its success, is the world's most successful and sophisticated cooperative economy. . . . Collectively, 8,000 cooperative enterprises account for 40 percent of the region's gross domestic product (GDP).[5]

Stewards of Enterprise

Margaret Lund is an independent consultant specializing in cooperatives with a particular interest in the impact and lessons from Emilia-Romagna. With Matt Hancock, a principal at Praxis Consulting Group in Philadelphia, who has lived, worked, and studied in Bologna, she wrote a lengthy and inspiring paper called "Stewards of Enterprise: Lessons in Economic Democracy from Northern Italy."[6] I recommend that you read it. You will be as moved as I was by one of the world's longest-running, most successful experiments in economic democracy. The paper has great breadth: sweeping history, strong social and economic theory, compelling storytelling, and vivid comparisons between something that truly works for people (the Emilia-Romagna economy and government) and something that doesn't (the US economy and government). It all starts with the birth of a regional restoration. Between 1945 and the late 1970s, Emilia-Romagna was transformed from a backward swampland with an impoverished economy to one of the most wealthy and equitable societies in Europe. The provincial government and labor unions collaborated with the region's association of cooperative enterprises to make this possible. Lund and Hancock say:

> Italy has one of the highest concentrations, per capita, of cooperative businesses in the world. . . . [They] employ 1.2 million people. . . . [They] are democratically governed and owned—not by wealthy families, private equity firms, multinational corporations or investors—but by the workers, farmers and consumers that live in this region. These firms have created wealth beyond the imagination of their forebears, in an industrial

model renowned for its nimbleness, high quality products, and merito-cratic approach. They have contributed to a local and regional political climate widely recognized for its honesty and efficiency.[7] Such an achievement of fairness and prosperity, rising wealth twinned with rising equal-ity, has seldom happened in the industrialized world, and never before for decade after decade, generation upon generation.[8]

After years of studying the Italian co-op experience, Margaret and Matt came to understand that they were studying a story of stewardship. They point to three core values of the democratic owners in this cooperative system:

Stewardship, agency, and *transparency* are fundamental to the success of each enterprise. Equally fundamental is the concept that these values ap-ply not just within each individual cooperative, but to the system of coop-eratives as a whole and their relationships to each other.[9]

Far from being on their own to figure out complex human resource problems, tax issues, industry trends, or real estate negotiations as Ameri-can entrepreneurs are, small cooperative businesses in Italy have access to a sophisticated support network to turn to at every juncture.[10]

Wouldn't all of us in business love to have such support? (Later in this chap-ter, you'll read about several organizations that are providing such support here in the United States.) An unusual aspect of the Emilia-Romagna support system is its devotion to its smaller members. The size of the system itself does not overwhelm the smaller businesses; in fact it nurtures them, lifts them up, and helps them to succeed as much as the larger businesses in the network.

The authors conclude with an eloquent statement of the results they observed:

What we see in the Italian cooperative system is as close to a true practice of economic democracy as is seen anywhere in the world. . . . [Economic de-mocracy] should be very familiar to us as Americans, because it effectively is a system where the things of which we are most proud are "indivisible," they happen from combined effort of all and belong to a united us—past, present and future. And it is a place with "liberty and justice for all."

The Emilia-Romagna Difference

In Emilia-Romagna, there are estimated to be more than three thousand employee-owned firms, mostly worker cooperatives. The Italian worker-owned firms range from a few dozen to a few thousand workers. They are more comparable in size to US ESOPs. The most successful of these co-ops have been employee-owned for decades; some are ninety years old or more. Most hire based on a cooperative spirit in addition to technical skills, and most are committed to succession planning and leadership development at all levels.

The most powerful government support comes in the form of not taxing profits set aside as "indivisible reserves." Indivisible reserves can be used to grow the co-op, but they can never be paid out to members. This has encouraged co-ops to set aside large percentages of their profits in this way. Interestingly, this practice long predates the law that incentivizes it. This is an example of co-ops making a business choice to prioritize future generations over current members and stakeholders.

There are other places in the world—besides Mondragon and Emilia-Romagna—where significant clusters of worker co-ops have dramatically altered economies. But at least one example in the United States appears to have the characteristics, aspirations, orientation, and energy to perhaps become the next Emilia-Romagna: The Industrial Commons in North Carolina.

THE INDUSTRIAL COMMONS

The Industrial Commons (TIC) is a nonprofit formed in 2015 in response to the need to rebuild wealth in rural western North Carolina. This region lost most of its substantial textile and furniture industries to offshoring. TIC launches and scales community-owned social enterprises and industrial cooperatives. It supports frontline workers to erase poverty inequities and build a more vibrant and inclusive local economy.

Molly Hemstreet and Sara Chester, who cofounded TIC and serve as joint executive directors, both grew up in Morganton, the small city where TIC is located. Both came home after college, Molly to teach and Sara to do economic development work. At the time, the area had lost forty thousand jobs in eight years.

Molly commented on how hard it is to teach children "when the fabric of an economy has been so completely pulled apart. That's when I became interested in the question of how we can rebuild wealth," she told me. While she was teaching, in 2008, she launched a company called Opportunity Threads, which has become the largest worker-owned cut-and-sew textile plant in the United States. "I had to put my house up to finance it. We had no money; my husband was in school, I was teaching and making $8 an hour, we were living hand to mouth." But Opportunity Threads thrived. When I spoke to her, the company had fifty workers. Most are owners, and they focus on reuse. "People send old T-shirts, and we upcycle them into new products. We process 70,000 T-shirts a week."

Meanwhile, Sara, in her economic development work, was seeing the same indications as Molly. The two of them met and started the Carolina Textile District (CTD)—a member-governed network of values-aligned producers in North and South Carolina—to help rebuild the local textile industry. During the COVID-19 pandemic, CTD was awarded a state contract to produce masks for North Carolina daycare facilities. No one small producer would have been able to land the contract. CTD was able to farm out $4 million of work to several factories during a critical time. The work was crucial to their survival. CTD would lead to the founding of The Industrial Commons, which has grown, thrived, and expanded its reach tremendously in recent years.

Aaron Dawson, TIC's senior director of training and development, leads efforts to create and sustain worker engagement programs in TIC enterprises and assists with employee ownership transitions. In our conversation, Aaron said, "We've been riding this powerful bike, but the Mount Everest we're about to climb is going to need more mechanics and a bigger engine. Molly and Sara have been the wheels that have moved us. Now we're at a point where we need to build out more components."

Ultimately, TIC will grow beyond its remarkably effective founders and twenty-five current employees. One growth indicator is the TIC Innovation Campus being built on a large brownfield site in downtown Morganton.

Reclaiming the Drexel Site

The twenty-eight-acre Drexel site has been a fixture of the Morganton community since the early 1900s. Generations of family members made some of the world's finest furniture here. At times, there were 2,400 Drexel workers on the site. When it closed its doors in 2001, it was the single largest employer in

Burke County. After a fire destroyed the factory in 2009, the land sat vacant and unkept for over thirteen years.

TIC had a bold idea: purchase the property and begin to plan an extraordinary project—the TIC Innovation Campus and an associated housing cooperative. The Innovation Campus will house small to midsize textile and furniture manufacturing firms, incubation space for emerging manufacturing businesses, art space, worker training and education facilities, recreation space, and TIC offices. It's a breathtaking array of interdependent programs and facilities.

On an adjacent acquisition of 10.3 acres, a housing cooperative with fifty-five units of workforce housing is planned. An unusual ownership structure, combining a limited equity cooperative with a community land trust, will ensure long-term affordability, modest wealth generation for individuals, and housing stability for the community. In addition, TIC is committed to high-performance, low-carbon campus construction and will try to achieve at least one aspect of the Living Building Challenge, the most rigorous and wholistic building certification program in the world. With everything else that TIC is tackling, I admire that they're committed to lofty building standards, but I'm not surprised—it seems that everything TIC does is infused with that degree of quality.

The campus planning is guided by a steering committee of local government and education entities, economic development organizations, and businesses. This is what TIC does so well—always integrating its activities with local and state government, educational programs, sympathetic funders, and existing community organizations. Reminiscent of Emilia-Romagna, this collaboration between the private and public sectors moves the region forward and creates a road map to support the next generation of American manufacturing.

Along with cooperative development work, education and workforce training, a campus, and a housing cooperative, TIC has also launched Capital for the Commons, a community loan fund to financially support the businesses TIC is creating.

Community Integration and Continuity

I asked Molly if she thought that the success of the community integration aspects of TIC is partly because she and Sara, the leaders of this effort, are locals who have been deeply embedded in the community since birth. "That part is huge," she said, "as is the co-directorship. We play off each other. We are starting to build out a team of leaders at TIC, and keeping those community connections strong is an important aspect of that." TIC is doing the kind of capacity-building that will be essential for future successions and organizational longevity.

Sara says that she and Molly have always focused on building social capital in the region—that has been a key factor in their success. Amy Vaughn, a recent hire at TIC (who graciously went to the Morganton library for me to find the Drexel site history), comments about this from her "fresh eyes" perspective: "Looking for partners and people who share your vision seems like a key to success. TIC's evolution into a regional change maker comes not from an opportunistic linear progression, but from the recognition of the importance of relationships and a commitment to finding people and partners who share the vision."

Another essential element of this new manufacturing ecosystem is the concept of *circularity*—products, resources, and services are recycled, composted, or reused in a way that brings them into a new life cycle or supply chain. The industries being created are designed to feed off each other's strengths, just as the TIC co-directors do. According to Carolyn Edsell-Vetter of the Cooperative Fund of the Northeast, "Few co-op funders or developers seem to understand this, particularly in the conversion space, where bigger firms are seen as the path to scale, rather than an ecosystem approach informed by permaculture, with interconnected and redundant nodes which combine to have a multiplier effect."

If TIC keeps aiming for the moon, keeps building great leadership, keeps scaling, and stays focused on long-term success, this institution may provide guidance for other regions in the United States. As Molly says, "There's a palpable renaissance happening in our community. This is what the future of work can look like and how imagination, creativity, and equity can influence the front lines of manufacturing work."

THE NAMASTE NETWORK

TIC is becoming a cooperative ecosystem by design and intention. Others can happen without a grand scheme.

With over two hundred employees and $40 million to $50 million in annual revenues, Namaste Solar in Colorado is among the largest worker co-ops in the

United States. Cofounder Blake Jones was working in the oil and gas industry in the late 1990s. His brother urged him to consider what he was doing and provoked a dramatic shift in Blake's thinking. He quit working for Halliburton, found a job in renewable energy, and did solar work in Nepal for three years. Returning to the United States, he hooked up with two partners. The three of them, after concluding that "there's gotta be a better way," founded Namaste Solar in 2005.

They were committed to the renewable energy transition and to better business—more honest and transparent, employee-owned, and dedicated to workplace democracy. They were highly egalitarian from the start (for a time, everyone earned the same salary) but were experiencing growing pains. They received many acquisition offers, as successful companies do, but they refused them all and took a different path: in 2010, they discovered the worker cooperative model, saw that it was right for Namaste, and converted. They were helped by Jason Wiener (the attorney we met in chapter 4, who left New York, moved to Colorado, and became Namaste's in-house general counsel).

Since then, Blake and others from Namaste have incubated the "Namaste Network" of cooperative enterprises, as it has come to be known. Wiener said to me, "It comes from the so-called 'Namaste MBA.' I was thinking how many people they've inspired, trained, educated, and exposed to a new way of doing things; it's got to be in the thousands by now."

A common topic of debate among Namaste co-owners was how quickly and how much to grow. How could they harness economies of scale without compromising their business model and culture? They found a way by forming the Amicus Solar Cooperative.

Amicus Solar Cooperative

Blake, Stephen Irvin, and their fellow co-owners at Namaste Solar recognized that national solar companies were taking over the solar installation industry and threatening the small independent solar companies who had less buying power. So they created an alternative. The Amicus Solar Cooperative is a purchasing cooperative that has recruited the most progressive and effective independent US and Canadian solar companies. Aggregated buying power helps them keep their footholds in an increasingly competitive market. They have joined forces to expand their ability to give their customers the best pricing and service.

But the members of Amicus do more for each other—they share best practices and help each other become better companies. South Mountain has been a long-time member, and I recall that the early gatherings of the Amicus group were compelling. The intelligence, the heart and soul, the culture of civility, humility, humor, inquiry, fellowship, and friendship at these gatherings is extraordinary.

And there is a contagion factor that has elevated us all. Today, there are eighty-two company members nationwide that have achieved the requirements for membership. Of these, according to Amicus CEO Stephen Irvin, twenty-four are benefit corporations, twenty are B Corps, and twenty-three are employee-owned. Júlia Martins Rodrigues and Nathan Schneider of the University of Colorado say, "By forming an independent purchasing co-op, the team behind Namaste Solar retained a locally grounded worker co-op while achieving impact at a national scale and beyond."[11]

But Blake and his colleagues were hardly done; there was plenty more to come.

Amicus O&M, Clean Energy Credit Union, and Kachuwa

By 2016, Amicus members recognized another challenge. Many had troubles fulfilling operations and maintenance (O&M) service contracts. By banding together and forming Amicus O&M Cooperative, led by longtime Namaste co-owner Amanda Bybee, the cooperative allows member companies to easily contract with each other and share best practices in this important aspect of their businesses.

The next hurdle was financing. The high up-front costs of solar projects often require loans, and Amicus members found the typical loan products to be insufficient to serve their less affluent clients. Amicus members created a new cooperative financial institution, the Clean Energy Credit Union, spearheaded by Blake, that would be owned by the consumers who are its depositors (unlike Namaste, which is owned by its workers, and Amicus, which is owned by its companies). Martins Rodrigues and Schneider write that "although the Clean Energy Credit Union is not controlled by Namaste Solar or the Amicus co-ops, it is part of a common ecosystem, with common leaders, and contributes to the shared objective of expanding the renewable energy market through values-driven business."[12]

Meanwhile, in 2005, Blake had founded the Kachuwa Impact Fund. Originally, it was a vehicle for him to invest his personal financial holdings in privately held companies that he admired for their positive impact. In 2016, he stepped down as CEO of Namaste Solar to expand Kachuwa and make it accessible to others looking for impact investments.

Today, Kachuwa (pronounced KAW-Chew-Ah) is a cooperative and benefit corporation with over $30 million in assets. Blake calls it "a Main Street mutual fund instead of a Wall Street mutual fund." It welcomes small investments and unaccredited investors, and it helps to fund all the things many of us would wish for: renewable energy, cooperatives, fair trade, affordable housing, sustainable forestry, organic food, and businesses owned or led by women and people of color.

"The Delaware of Cooperative Law"

Colorado has also advanced the co-op legal, policy, and regulatory cause. Democratic governor Jared Polis is a big supporter of employee ownership. Jason Wiener says that "in 2021, we passed the richest tax credit in the country for employee ownership conversions. It was expanded in 2023, and it's the first in the country to legally define and codify the substantive elements of employee ownership." Then, in 2024, legislation was passed to make the state center permanent, provide technical assistance, and expand tax credits, including a $50,000 tax credit to offset costs for employee ownership conversions.

Many cooperative businesses physically located elsewhere have chosen to incorporate in Colorado, leading Wiener and his colleague Linda Phillips to brand it "the Delaware of Cooperative Law." They have even trademarked this phrase that Jason says is "spreading like wildfire."

The network that Blake and Namaste Solar have built includes one of the largest worker co-ops in the United States, nationwide purchasing power, a financial network for both solar consumers and aligned businesses, and policy enhancements that have derived from these efforts. According to Martins Rodrigues and Schneider of the University of Colorado, "It's an ingenious design, if it had been designed from the start. But it was not."[13]

Blake, in his ever-modest way, says that they had no grand plan to create an ecosystem like Mondragon; they just kept seeing needs and filling them, one by one. The "emphasis remains the same as it was in the beginning," Blake told me. "Qualitative impact is more important to us than quantitative impact."

Apparently, the true visionaries in these endeavors—the Mollys and the Saras and the Blakes and the Stephens—are never willing to sacrifice quality for quantity. It's not necessary. And even in those places where these ecosystems have flourished, like Mondragon and Emilia-Romagna, the quality/quantity balance holds steady. As Martins Rodrigues and Schneider write:

> As it sought to balance environmental impact, survival, and growth, over time Namaste Solar incubated a national-scale ecosystem through a series of sibling co-operatives. . . . Together, they have contributed to reshaping their industry nationally.[14]

They further point out that this kind of cooperation between worker co-ops, purchasing cooperatives, and a credit union is extremely rare in the US context, which makes this constellation more powerful in demonstrating how different types of cooperatives can mutually reinforce each other using various stakeholder designs that are appropriate to filling each need.

BUILDING ENERGY BOTTOM LINES

The Amicus contagion factor—companies deciding to become employee-owned because of their proximity with others that are—is important, and I think it may become more prevalent. Here's another early example of that factor.

Climate change was the inspiration for Building Energy Bottom Lines, one of the suite of programs that operate under the "Building Energy" banner of the Northeast Sustainable Energy Association (NESEA). NESEA's membership consists primarily of architecture, engineering, building, and renewable energy professionals and businesses dedicated to high-performance building and carbon reduction.

NESEA member businesses, including South Mountain, recognized that their technical and policy proficiencies had increased but their businesses were not keeping pace. So, they organized Building Energy Bottom Lines (BEBL) as a regional peer network of building industry professionals. The purpose was to share triple-bottom-line business practices and increase business effectiveness to make a greater impact on climate change.

BEBL began in 2014 with thirty architecture, building, and design/build firms organized in three groups, each with a skilled paid facilitator. Today, there are seventy businesses in seven groups. The latest groups, funded by a grant from a Massachusetts government agency, consist of women-owned companies and companies owned by people of color. The scale of the individual businesses varies, from very small to more than one hundred employees. Each cohort gathers twice a year for intensive two-day sessions and communicates online year-round. All companies meet together periodically at full network gatherings.

The fundamental purpose of BEBL is to foster broad-based mastery of *business skills* to complement and support our *technical skills*—to pay equal attention to the craft of business as to technology and building science. We need to build strong businesses as well as great buildings; in fact, we are unlikely to succeed at one without the other. Bottom Lines offers a place for deep introspection with trusted peers to expand the business and leadership skills and capacities of every member.

An especially compelling aspect of Bottom Lines is the way it works. Companies in the various cohorts lay their practices on the table in fully transparent ways to help each other become more effective businesses. Early on, our only fear was that extensive territory overlap might lead to competition issues between companies. Our remarkable finding, ten years in, is that the problem we imagined has never surfaced, and the extensive information sharing has only led to valuable collaborations which otherwise may not have occurred.

Although this ethos of cooperation is apparently on the rise, it is still missing in much of US business. Have we been so convinced by American individualism that we can't see the benefits of cooperation? Are we so fearful that we worry that sharing information will lead to losing it?

Because of the triple-bottom-line focus, there is significant attention paid to business structure, succession, and equity. When BEBL formed, there were two employee-owned companies among its members. Today, there are about a dozen, with another dozen or so conversions underway and many others considering it. Wherever the model is accessible and available, it seems, the model spreads. In this case, mission-driven member companies like Byggmeister, New

Energy Works (the largest BEBL company), Wolfworks, Trillium Architects, Maine Passive House, and others have made employee ownership conversions.

A new offshoot of BEBL has just formed in the Pacific Northwest. Another is being contemplated in North Carolina. It's clear that this peer support system, a learning co-op of sorts, fills a need and will hopefully continue to spread. It's likely to inspire more employee-owned companies as its members learn by example.

ICA GROUP SECONDARY COOPERATIVES

ICA Group, the nonprofit that has been one of the leading worker co-op conversion organizations for decades, has also become a leader in the development of industry-specific cooperatives of worker co-ops (known as secondary cooperatives).

ICA is in the process of launching Elevate, a national cooperative of home care worker co-ops. Katrina Kazda, the ICA vice president of home care innovations and lead developer of Elevate, told me that "joining together through collective voice and action, home care cooperatives can increase profits, benefits and pay; invest in advanced training and on-the-job supports; increase the growth and scale of the home care cooperative sector; and push for necessary policy change."

The sector currently includes twenty-one worker co-ops, in ten states and Puerto Rico, employing over 2,200 home care workers. ICA also launched Co-Rise Cooperative in 2019, a secondary cooperative supporting family childcare workers.

MODELS FOR THE REST OF THE WORLD

Cooperative clusters are increasing in numbers. Some of them have mighty impact. Japan is one of the world's leading fishing nations. It's a little-known fact that Japan's fishing industry is entirely organized on a cooperative basis, with 2,500 fishing cooperatives nationwide.

In John Restakis' book, *Humanizing the Economy*, he says:

[Japan's fishing co-ops] are responsible for the management of all aspects of fishing including the provision of banking and credit, the supply and sale of gear, fuel, ice, food and other daily necessities, mutual insurance and welfare, transportation, wholesale operations and the processing, storage and sale of catches and fish products. One of their most important functions, however, is to monitor and implement regulatory practices related to managing fish stocks. . . . This locally-controlled system, based on the twin principles of equity and collective responsibility, has been the world's prime example of how to successfully and cooperatively manage a fishing commons.[15]

It is an extraordinary system with a mighty impact, a model for the rest of the world—like Mondragon, Emilia-Romagna, TIC, and the Namaste Network.

There are other impressive and promising cooperative networks in operation and formation in the United States. They include nonprofits like Co-op Cincy in Cincinnati, Cooperative Economic Network of Detroit, MadWorC in Madison, and cooperatives of cooperatives like the Arizmendi Association of Cooperatives in Northern California. Another model with great potential is cooperative holding companies, which are examined in chapter 8.

This chapter has illustrated what you can do to increase the impact of your own Five Transitions work. By aligning with other cooperative businesses, you can enhance your own business, create support networks for others, and increase community ownership and wealth. I hope it has helped you recognize the breadth of possibilities that can build steam once the cooperative bug bites.

CHAPTER 6

THE ESOP CONUNDRUM

I f you mention "employee ownership" to any business owner, adviser, accountant, attorney, or financial planner, an "ESOP" is likely to be the first thing that comes to their mind. Go ahead, try it with someone you know in one of those categories. Ask them, "What kinds of employee ownership are you familiar with?" Odds are that the term will be in the first sentence of their response.

Not surprising. Employee stock ownership plans (ESOPs) are by far the most common and well-known form of employee ownership in the United States. There are roughly 6,500 such plans serving more than 14 million employees.[1] As John Case, coauthor of *Ownership*, said to me, "A single ESOP might employ more people than all the US co-ops combined, and ESOPs distribute many times more wealth." (That is certainly true in the United States, but not worldwide.)

WHAT IS AN ESOP, ANYWAY?

ESOPs are tax-advantaged qualified retirement plans used to transfer the shares in a private company to a trust on behalf of the employees. They were invented by Louis Kelso, an economist and lawyer, to allow working people to buy stock in the company that employs them and pay for it out of the company's future income. In 1956, Kelso created the first ESOP for the purpose of transitioning the ownership of Peninsula Newspapers, Inc., from its elderly founders to their chosen successors—the company's employees.

In 1974, the US Congress passed the Employee Retirement Income Security Act (ERISA) to govern all voluntarily established private-sector retirement and health plans. One area of that is the protection of the interests of employees in retirement plans that are used to transfer the company shares to a trust on behalf of the employees—which is what an ESOP does. The ESOP is a form of employee ownership that exists only in the United States.

Because ESOPs are expensive to establish and maintain because of regulatory requirements, they are rarely appropriate for companies with fewer than forty employees and $10 million in annual revenues. That is my own assessment; others feel that smaller companies can become ESOPs if they have very strong cash flow and high profitability.

Employees are not direct shareholders. The shares are held in a trust with the employees as beneficiaries and are paid out when they leave the company or retire, at which point the company repurchases the shares. The stock held in the ESOP must be valued independently on an annual basis.

There are many ESOP versions and manifestations. They are fundamentally different creatures from worker co-ops, but occasionally the lines can get blurry, as it does with Once Again Nut Butter.

ONCE AGAIN NUT BUTTER

In 1976, Jeremy Thaler and Constance Potter, two hippie entrepreneurs who had a history of starting co-ops, began making peanut butter in their basement in tiny Nunda, New York, about an hour south of Rochester. People said, "Once again, they're starting a business," and Once Again Nut Butter had its name. In 1981, they left the basement, bought a rundown turn-of-the-century silk processing factory in town, and renovated it for nut butter production.

Long before Jeremy's death in 2012 and Connie's departure from the business, they converted the company to an ESOP in 1998. In 2006, it became 100 percent employee-owned, and they completed a next-generation leadership change. Bob Gelser became CEO in 2007, and Larry Filipsky became CFO in 2013.

When I spoke to Bob and Larry in March 2024, the company had one hundred employees and more than $60 million in annual gross revenues. They had just opened a second plant in the Central Valley of California, where all US commercial almonds are grown (and 82 percent of the almonds in the world). As Larry says, "The almonds are shipped to our New York plant, made into almond butter, and a large percentage is shipped right back to California. Might as well make some butter out there."

Before coming to Once Again, both Bob and Larry had worked at Stone Construction Equipment in nearby Honeoye, New York. Larry says, "CEO Bob Fein took a typical management versus labor type company and turned it into a phenomenal ESOP. He built an incredible culture. The stories I could tell you about people going above and beyond are unbelievable." The story of Stone Construction is told with inspiring detail by Corey Rosen, John Case, and Martin Staubus in their book *Equity*.

Even though it wasn't *actually* a co-op, Jeremy and Connie always ran Once Again like a worker co-op, with each person having a vote on matters of importance. In fact, Bob chuckles, "Jeremy called it a worker co-op—*and* an ESOP!— till the day he died."

When Jeremy prepared to retire, he began the task of replacing himself. He hired a general manager who didn't work out. Then he brought Bob Gelser onto the Once Again board and asked him to serve on the search committee. Their second hire was a failure, too. Jeremy asked Bob to throw his hat in the ring for the job. Bob says, "I was humbled to be asked, but to be honest, I was a bit scared, and I declined." They went through another recruiting effort.

They had candidates, and Bob went to a board meeting expecting a discussion about the applicants. To his surprise, when he got there, they didn't want to hire any of them. Instead, the board asked him what it would take for him to take the job as CEO. Bob felt more confident and this time he did not turn them down.

The six-person board is comprised of three employees and three external members. "The internal board members," Bob says, "tend to be line employees, not management."

I asked why there is an even number of board members. Couldn't that be problematic when there's a contested issue? Bob feels that the structure incentivizes board members to find solutions. He says, "There have been some four to two votes, but never a tie. When something's close, you work harder to find a way through it."

They also have one external trustee, appointed by the board, whose responsibilities are to (a) select a valuation firm and oversee the ERISA-required annual company evaluation that determines stock price; and (b) oversee vote counts, ratify board member elections, and tend to the state's other statutory requirements. They are legally required to act in the best interest of the ESOP participants.

Since Larry retired in 2022, Bob has begun to think about his own future retirement, and the company is thinking about its next succession. It's hard to attract talent to a tiny rural town in upstate New York. They're working to develop the right internal talent, but that's no sure bet. Once Again pays competitive wages, but they shine on benefits and the large contributions they make to the ESOP, which is gradually increasing its share value. When we spoke, the shares were worth $250, and some employee-owners have earned as many as five thousand shares.

"So, you're making millionaires, right?" I asked.

"Yes," said Bob, "As of last Monday there were seven. And some of the biggest accounts are production people who have been here a long time." People retire, their shares are repurchased, and they walk out the door with quite a nest egg.

In a town of three thousand, the local economy is tremendously uplifted by this company. It has a large number of employees (second only to the school district), and its profits (derived from revenue that comes from all over the country) create widespread local wealth.

Alex Moss, the founder of Praxis Consulting Group in Philadelphia, has had a long association with Once Again. He ran their 2023 board retreat and learned for the first time that the company had never been a worker co-op. But, he said, "If you look at their voting and legal structure, you see a lot of embedded worker co-op sensibility, perhaps more than in any ESOP I know." A comprehensive decision-making matrix makes it clear which decisions are made by whom. Different decisions are made by board members, ESOP members, ESOP trustees, and employees who have completed the probation period. Operational decisions are made by management.

In my view, Once Again is everything that an ESOP can and should be. It has shared ownership, transparency, employee engagement, and social commitment and takes long-term mission protection further than most ESOPs. It embodies all the characteristics of a CommonWealth company. It satisfies three of the Five Transitions, and while Once Again is not, as of now, a B Corp, it easily could be.

NCEO AND ESOP INFRASTRUCTURE

As a staff member in the US Senate in the 1970s, Corey Rosen worked on drafting ESOP legislation. In 1981, he founded the National Center for Employee Ownership (NCEO), a nonprofit membership organization that advocates for and supports the employee ownership community. NCEO has been a tremendous force in employee ownership education. Although it works on behalf of all major forms of employee ownership, its primary focus has been on ESOPs.

The other major organization promoting this form of employee ownership is the ESOP Association. Founded in 1991, it is the primary ESOP policy and lobbying voice and works to refine and improve the ESOP regulatory apparatus, promote legislation, and spread best practices.

There's also the Employee-Owned S-Corporations of America (ESCA), whose sole purpose is to protect the ESOP S-Corp preferential tax treatment. Beyond these organizations, there is an entire industry of attorneys, accountants, valuators, and other service providers that has grown up to support the creation and maintenance of ESOPs.

Performance and Expansion

ESOPs tend to outperform conventional companies in a variety of ways. Ownership stakes motivate employees to higher levels of productivity, profitability, engagement, loyalty, and long-term value creation. ESOPs can give companies an advantage in attracting talent, not only because of the ownership opportunity but because wages are higher and retirement savings grow faster.

In the book *Ownership*, the authors note that "a study by the Democracy Collaborative found that 20 employee-owned B Corporations outperformed 20 similar but not employee-owned companies by 21 percent on B Lab's assessment tool." They go on to say that ESOPs also have higher survival rates, pointing to a study tracking such companies over ten years that found that privately held employee-owned companies were half as likely as nonemployee-owned companies to go bankrupt or close.[2]

Wanting to expand employee ownership nationally, NCEO created a task force in 2016 to expand the number of state centers for employee ownership, of which there were about ten at that time. With the help of the NCEO State

Center Task Force, a few Pennsylvania business owners and service providers, led by Ken Baker of New Age Industries and Jim Steiker of SES ESOP Strategies, helped to start the Pennsylvania Center for Employee Ownership (PACEO).

Based on the success of the PACEO, Ken, Jim, and a few other individuals formed the Employee Ownership Expansion Network (EOX), a national nonprofit whose sole mission is to open and support new state centers. In 2019, EOX hired Steve Storkan, an ESOP service provider, to be the organization's first executive director. As of June 2024, there were employee ownership centers in twenty-three states. These centers have become an important part of the US employee ownership infrastructure, providing essential services and assistance to business owners interested in conversion.

Key Policy Issues

Loren Rodgers, NCEO's executive director since 2011 (when founder Corey Rosen stepped out of the daily management role), says a key current policy issue is to convince the US Department of Labor to allocate significant funds to these rapidly spreading statewide centers under the WORK Act. (WORK is short for the Worker Ownership and Readiness and Knowledge Act, the awkward name for excellent legislation passed by Congress and President Joseph Biden in February 2023, largely due to the efforts of Senator Bernie Sanders of Vermont.)

A second key policy issue is creating legislation that would certify employee-owned companies whose owners are women or minorities so that they can take advantage of federal programs and contract preferences for those demographics. "I would love it if the requirements to be a certified minority- or women-owned business allowed one to look *through* the ESOP to the ESOP participants," says Loren. "One of our member companies is a hundred percent ESOP owned. More than half of those shares are owned by Latinx workers, but they don't qualify as minority-owned because the ESOP itself doesn't have any race or gender."

Meanwhile, as NCEO and others expand the appeal and practice of employee ownership, there are many reasons an owner might sell to an ESOP. The employees who helped build the business get the reward of ownership. The seller is paid the business's fair value, as determined by a third-party valuator. If emphasized, employee engagement, participation, and productivity may grow. It's a way for owners to ensure that the company will remain independent, unlike selling to a strategic buyer or private equity.

As the next section shows, it is not always the case that ESOPs continue to be independent in the long term, but many do, and it is a widespread aspiration in the ESOP community.

THE NEW BELGIUM FACTOR

For many years, the New Belgium Brewery (NBB) in Fort Collins, Colorado, starred as an emblematic ESOP that built a superb workplace culture of open-book management, employee engagement, environmental sustainability, and shared ownership. NBB is a B Corp leader, has been a pioneer of good business, and is a model for both the craft brewing industry and the ESOP community. NBB institutionalized the kind of co-op behaviors exemplified by Once Again Nut Butter.

In 2019, cofounder Kim Jordan announced that the company would be sold to a subsidiary of Japanese beverage giant Kirin Holdings and would no longer be an ESOP. The sale rocked the employee ownership world just as the sale of Ben and Jerry's rocked the socially responsible business movement nearly twenty years before.

With over seven hundred employees and revenues of more than $300 million, NBB was 100 percent owned by the ESOP. Roughly three hundred employees owned shares at the time of the sale. The shareholders approved the sale, with each receiving at least $100,000 and some much more. Because of New Belgium's high profile, the sale of the company and the end of its ESOP has drawn significant attention.

Jessica Rose, director of employee ownership programs at the Democracy Collaborative, said at the time:

> New Belgium's success as a mission-led business that shaped an entire industry made me proud to be a part of the movement to promote employee ownership. So, like many of my peers, I felt a real sense of loss when I woke up to read about the acquisition. Is the outcome of this

corporate buyout a success story, in which hundreds of rank-and-file worker-owners now have a . . . chance to benefit their families and communities in a way that few middle-class Americans are afforded? Or is it merely a failure that illustrates the insurmountable gravitational pull of wealth-concentration in a capitalist system? What does it say that even the most integral moral commitment to worker equity ultimately could not stand up to economic and market pressures?[3]

It's not rare for ESOPs to be purchased and absorbed by larger companies, at which point employee ownership usually ends.

Alex Moss of Praxis Consulting Group, which mostly works with ESOPs, is a strong believer in the value of the model, but he said to me:

> There's leakage at the bottom of the barrel—not for failure, but for success. Many ESOP companies get offers they can't refuse, and they sell. Those who are concerned tend to take steps to develop active board policies on how to respond to unsolicited purchase offers. The idea is to avoid being dragged into selling for the wrong reasons, or without having thought it through very carefully, and always to be looking through the lens of what's best for the ESOP plan participants.

Later in this chapter we'll meet ReVision Energy, a company that has taken Alex's advice.

The ESOP trustee has the fiduciary responsibility to act on behalf of the participants and sometimes recommends a sale, but Alex feels that the decision should never get to the trustee unless the board of directors makes that recommendation. Protections against acquisition can be built in, and Praxis works hard to do that with its clients.

The protections do not always succeed, however, or they don't exist in many cases, and that has become a conundrum in the ESOP world. The NBB sale provoked a variety of reactions among employee ownership advocates.

Jason Wiener, the Colorado attorney, sees benefits and detriments. "Only good things came from the New Belgium experiment, *except* that it didn't last.

The sale could send hundreds of former employees—well trained in how business can work and the benefits of employee ownership—out into the economy to make better businesses. We'll see if that comes to pass. At least New Belgium has succeeded at its purpose of creating wealth for employees."

Wealth for only some of them, I would add. Three hundred employees received windfalls, which could mean a new home, a college education for the kids, or a sizable retirement contribution. Or new responsible business creations, as Jason suggests. But what about the rest who were not yet plan participants? They received no windfall, and they have no more ESOP to join. Neither do future employees. Alex Moss says there is a lively discussion in the ESOP world today about boards and trustees taking future employees into account during their deliberations.

Dave Hammer, executive director of the ICA Group, advocates for more permanence: "While employee ownership is a great boon for millions of workers, when it is merely a way station, we lose an opportunity to leverage our collective power to make real transformative change in our society."[4]

Jen Briggs was the NBB vice president of human resources for 13 years. She was, perhaps, the person most responsible for building the open ownership culture that made NBB into an exemplary CommonWealth company. As I've emphasized, ESOP ownership doesn't necessarily lead to those values. Jen says the ESOP was part of their success, but that an ESOP itself does not itself create a culture and company like New Belgium. Jen says that it was what she calls "an integrated impact culture" that made it special. And she has anecdotal evidence that various former employees have incorporated these ideals into their work as leaders in new companies and starting their own small businesses, as Jason Wiener suggested they might.

New Belgium was a local business in Fort Collins, Colorado and Asheville, North Carolina, serving its community and creating shared wealth for its many employee-owners. "But it was also a national brand struggling to survive in a cut-throat landscape," says Jen Briggs. Finally, selling to a multinational and disbanding the ESOP was a complex decision that included factors like the competitive marketplace and conditions in the US economy that favor consolidation and vertical integration."

In the early days, they believed that becoming an ESOP would enhance the superb employee engagement culture they had built, but they eventually discovered it was a "poison pill" that would not allow them to continue to practice their mission, culture, and values. Overall, that must count as a loss. But I'm not one of those employee-owners who left with new wealth, so it's easy for me to say.

After having talked to many people on this subject, I'm not convinced I fully understand the nuances of the real story. But I know this: there is no longer an ESOP. Future employees (along with those who were not owners at the time of the sale) are unrewarded.

In terms of durability and longevity, ESOPs are vulnerable.

EMPOWERED VENTURES

Empowered Ventures (EV) in Indiana models a way to turn that vulnerability around. EV is an ESOP holding company. It identifies strong companies that would be attractive to private equity, purchases them from exiting owners for market value, provides capital and management expertise, amalgamates them so that each can provide support to the others, and holds ownership, with no intent to ever sell. In a 2024 Vermont Employee Ownership Center blog post, the authors say:

> The ESOP holding company offers a promising alternative, aiming to hold ownership of the companies they acquire over the long-term, supporting their growth from a healthy distance, and giving all employees at those companies an equity stake in the full ESOP portfolio. If there's a different model that could hope to compete with the momentum of private equity acquisitions, this may be it.[5]

In chapter 8, I provide other examples of innovative new organizations whose goal is to provide an alternative to predatory private equity. Although Empowered Ventures belongs with those, I include it in this chapter because it is specifically designed to be an antidote to the ESOP conundrum.

REVISION ENERGY

Most ESOPs do not exemplify this book's Five Transitions. They do satisfy the most important one by sharing ownership, but that is not necessarily a long-term condition, as we have seen. ESOPs certainly have second-generation leadership (many), participatory management and governance (a few), and B Corp certification (relatively few). But even for those inclined toward the Five Transitions, the mission preservation question remains. Some notable ESOP examples with CommonWealth characteristics are Johnny's Selected Seeds in Maine; King Arthur Baking, Gardener's Supply, and Carris Reels in Vermont; New Energy Works in New York and Oregon; Hypertherm in New Hampshire; New Age Industries in Pennsylvania; Bob's Red Mill Foods in Oregon; and Stone Age Inc. in Colorado.

Sun Light and Power in California is an example of an ESOP that has institutionalized and combined the best of the ESOP and the worker co-op and calls itself an "Esoperative" (and now, with B Corp certification, a "Besoperative").

And then there's ReVision Energy, an ESOP that has achieved the Five Transitions as well as any company I know, except for the lingering doubt about its susceptibility to purchase.

Located in Maine and with satellite offices and operations in New Hampshire and Massachusetts, ReVision has more than five hundred employees and annual revenues in excess of $170 million. I think it's fair to say that ReVision is the premier solar and carbon reduction company in New England. (I add "carbon reduction" after "solar" because in addition to designing and installing solar electric systems, ReVision provides electric vehicle charging, battery storage, and beneficial electrification for building HVAC and hot water). The clientele is residential, commercial, institutional, and municipal.

The president of the company, forty-eight-year-old Fortunat Mueller, is the second youngest of the four partners who started the business together in 2003. Dan Clapp is a few years younger, Phil Coupe ten years older, and Bill Behrens ten years older than Phil.

When we spoke in February 2024, Fortunat told me about a sabbatical from work he was planning with his family, which he felt would be important for both the family and for ReVision. He is excited about seeing Africa and Europe and showing his daughters that rural Maine is not the whole planet. He is excited about his first extended break from the company since its founding and equally excited about the potential impact of his absence on the company and his plans when returning. "I've still got a lot of tread on my tires here," he says.

ReVision has grown steadily during its twenty-plus years in business, but according to Fortunat:

> Growth for its own sake has never been our priority. We frame growth around the environmental imperative in this way—the world needs a lot of what we do; we think we do it pretty well; and therefore we should deliver as much of it as we can, but only while being sure to maintain the rest of our values and [taking] care of all our stakeholders.

Individual opportunities also play a role in growth imperatives. "We want people to experience ReVision as a place to spend their whole career," Fortunat said. Managed growth can provide people with the potential for varying company roles over time.

The ReVision ESOP

ReVision became an ESOP in 2017. The four partners realized that, given their age differences, they would probably phase out at different times. An attractive aspect of doing an early ESOP conversion was to separate the capital transition from the leadership transition so that each could occur on appropriate timelines. This is the get-the-ownership-thing-done-with-a-long-runway-to-the-leadership-transition approach that I have advocated previously.

Since the ESOP was formed, Bill has retired and now chairs the board. Phil is beginning to ease into transition. With the ESOP, they don't have to think about raising money to buy out interests or about what's fair and for whom. It's codified, the share price is known, and they have gone to great lengths to ensure that the money is available. Meanwhile, they have begun to prepare for a leadership succession in a gradual and measured way.

ReVision has three outside board members. Technically, it's four, if you count Bill. For many years, the structure was simple—the four founders effectively functioned as the board. When the ESOP transition happened, they formally created a board of directors that then consisted of the four founders plus their general counsel, who was a full-time employee and senior leader.

According to Fortunat, "We financed the ESOP purchase primarily with sellers' notes, so the four of us are guaranteed board seats until the note is extinguished." But when Bill stepped away from day-to-day management, they began to invest more rigor in the board and became more deliberate about its workings.

For the transaction, they had an external trustee, but they converted this role into an internal trustee committee of three. The trustee committee has a fiduciary responsibility separate from management. The committee's primary responsibilities are to review and accept the annual share valuation (making sure that it is good for the ESOP), elect board members (who in turn hire management), and vet any offers to buy the company.

I asked Fortunat if he was concerned about the New Belgium scenario happening at ReVision:

Yes, especially since we are just about to finish paying off the sellers' notes. We think that if we continue to be a profitable business, we can be an attractive acquisition target. We've begun writing some board and trustee policies that stipulate that we don't even have to consider an offer unless it looks like XYZ. We're making it very onerous for others to buy and for ReVision to sell.

He added that this is a very big question internally: Whose interests should the trustees represent? Is it only the current shareholders, or is it all the potential future shareholders, too? He thinks that's the most interesting issue the New Belgium sale brought up. "Wholistically," he says, "the point of the employee ownership structure is employee wealth generation, good wages and benefits, meaningful work and lifetime careers, and healthy retirement savings—all of it together comprises our purpose. Maintaining all these good things longterm is worthwhile and essential to our success."

Fortunat and his partners knew little or nothing about this acquisition aspect when they became an ESOP. Clearly, though, the New Belgium experience has influenced the thinking of some ESOP owners, and it's also apparent that

ReVision is part of the discussion of future ESOP owners that Alex Moss spoke about.

After eight years, Fortunat and his partners are satisfied with their decision to become an ESOP and with the kind of thinking and practices it has reinforced. "There are challenges," he says, "but I think we have deep buy-in from the vast majority of co-owners. I feel good that we are actively fighting against the inequality that exists in our world and creating opportunities for a broad array of co-owners in different roles."

Workforce Development

ReVision encourages an ownership mentality to seep into everything. The leadership team welcomes ideas coming from all parts of the company, about all aspects of the company, rather than ideas for improvements being siloed into particular areas of expertise or departments. One thing that supports this openness and cross-pollination is highly intentional and active workforce development. ReVision runs an internal leadership training program that distinguishes between positional power, reputational power, expertise power, and relational power and, Fortunat says, "how those things exist in different people at different times and how we have to name them and understand them."

A diverse group of co-owners go through ten weeks of leadership training in cohorts of twenty. At this point, a large percentage of employees have been through this program. A management training program follows the same model, and there are twelve-month apprentice programs for various disciplines.

ReVision has taken this work outside the company as well, partnering with other Maine organizations to do pre-apprentice electrical training. According to Fortunat:

There's a significant population of recent West African asylum seekers in the Portland area. So, we partnered with Portland Adult Ed to create a green energy program that would ultimately earn them a set of construction credentials, which could make them attractive employees. The first cohort was eighteen people; it was an amazing group of people. At the end, we hired four of them, and at least ten others were hired by our competitors and collaborators after we did a job fair with other solar, heat pump, and weatherization contractors.

ReVision did a similar partnership with Learning Works, an organization for kids for whom traditional high school doesn't work. These programs serve ReVision, and they serve the greater community of which it is a part.

The Vision

I asked Fortunat about his long-term vision for ReVision. His response was elegant (though I've edited his comments for the sake of brevity):

Our mission says it—*to make life better by building our just and equitable electric future.* But there's more. As we contribute meaningfully to the New England renewables transition, we also want to hold ourselves out as a beacon for a different way of running a private business—to let people know that we've succeeded *because* of our multi-stakeholder engagement, not *despite* it. We want to become "the most respected employee-owned company in the country," which would mean we've fully baked our values into the organization in a truly durable and authentic way.

Do not doubt for a moment that this won't all happen. Fortunat says, "I love talking about this stuff, but it's exhausting because I'm an introvert." But it's more than talk. He and his partners have created a powerful model for the rest of us about how business can truly be a force for good and build toward an economy that works for all. I predict that the ReVision version will last far longer than the New Belgium model which paved the way.

THE CONUNDRUM

The ESOP conundrum is actually a wider business conundrum. At issue are how to encourage more democratic ESOPs that are truly led by values, like Once Again Nut Butter and ReVision, and how to preserve values and purpose in the long term.

Each employee ownership model can potentially be used to do Five Transitions work and democratize. That includes ESOPs. However, ERISA is a big obstacle to ESOP mission protection. Its regulatory constraints deserve careful consideration when designing an ESOP conversion. As Dave Hammer of ICA Group said in a 2024 email, "Given that dozens, if not hundreds of ESOPs are 'demutualized' every year, locking future generations from ownership, it's something we have to take seriously."

CHAPTER 7

EMPLOYEE OWNERSHIP TRUSTS

While the worker cooperative must overcome misunderstandings about branding and leadership, and fear of democracy, and while the employee stock ownership plan (ESOP) must address concerns about complex regulations, high costs, and vulnerability to forced sales, the employee ownership trust (EOT)—an ascendant form of employee ownership—appears to suffer from none of these issues. So far, anyway.

Trusts are mechanisms used in our society for asset management and legal protection in a variety of ways. This chapter describes a few particular kinds of trusts and primarily the EOT, which is a mechanism by which an owner sells a company to a trust with the requirement that the trust will operate the company in the long term for the benefit of all its employees.

Although widespread in the United Kingdom, the EOT is relatively new to the United States. There are currently fewer than one hundred US EOTs. Unlike ESOPs and worker co-ops, EOTs do not build equity for the employees. Like an ESOP, the employees are beneficiaries of the trust, but the nature of the trust is different in important ways. In most cases, the profits, above those needed for reinvestment in the business, are distributed to the employee members of the trust as cash bonuses or are used to benefit the employees' interests in other ways. The point is not to accumulate value for the future, as it is with an ESOP and most worker co-ops, but rather to pay value to the employees as it's earned.

Since US EOTs are a relatively recent development, terms and definitions are in flux, prompting discussion and debate among practitioners and academics. Before we continue, here are a few related terms and the meaning I assign to them in this book:

- A "purpose trust" is an umbrella term used to describe any trust designed to ensure that a company functions to benefit one or more purposes (e.g., employee interests, or a particular mission).
- A perpetual purpose trust (PPT) is a specific type of purpose trust whose beneficiary is the company's mission rather than its owners, employees, or investors.
- An employee ownership trust (EOT) is a specific type of purpose trust whose beneficiaries are the employees of the company.

TRUSTS TO BENEFIT MISSION

Let's start with a brief look at perpetual purpose trusts. There are some noteworthy US examples.

In 2018, the Organically Grown Company (OGC) was a forty-year-old mission-driven company dedicated to better food and agricultural practices. It had become one of the largest US distributors of organic produce and a powerful activist in the industry. For ten years, OGC had been an ESOP and was able to fund share repurchases when employee-owners retired. But with many owners approaching retirement, the company became concerned about its ability to fund future retirements while also being able to invest in the business and maintain its mission-related priorities.

Natalie Reitman-White was vice president of organizational vitality and trade advocacy at OGC. She led an effort to buy back all the company shares and transfer them to the Sustainable Food and Agriculture Perpetual Purpose Trust to protect the company's economic, social, and environmental impact in perpetuity. All stakeholders—employees, farmers, customers, investors, and community members—now are represented by trustees who control the fate and future of the company. In a 2018 article, OGC CEO Elizabeth Nardi was quoted as saying, "Placing the company into a Purpose Trust ensures that we stay focused on our mission as [our] North Star, share real-time rewards with our stakeholders, and have aligned financing to increase our impact."[1] Wouldn't it have been something if New Belgium Brewery had known about the PPT option and taken this route?

While OGC was making the trust, Natalie learned that Oregon laws did not allow perpetual purpose trusts, so it was set up in Delaware. Since then, with her help and the leadership of Susan Gary, a University of Oregon law professor, Oregon has passed a law that establishes what they call "stewardship trusts" (essentially the same as a PPT) as a business option in that state.

When the effort to create a PPT for Organically Grown was complete, Natalie then formed Purpose Owned, an organization that helps companies to become EOTs and PPTs, and she continues to actively engage in this work.

Several other companies now also use a PPT to benefit a particular purpose. Notable among these is the widely publicized sale of outdoor clothing retailer Patagonia to a trust to benefit the environment in perpetuity—the planet is the sole beneficiary. Another, which Natalie helped develop, is the Zingerman's Community of Businesses PPT, which was layered onto an existing employee ownership program to specifically protect, in perpetuity, intellectual property and Zingerman's commitment to the local community of Ann Arbor, Michigan.

TRUSTS TO BENEFIT EMPLOYEES

While some purpose trusts take the form of PPTs, most take the form of EOTs, with their purpose being to specifically benefit the employees of the company while also maintaining the mission.

To convert to an EOT, a business owner creates the trust structure in collaboration with a legal professional, and the EOT then purchases from the owner all the shares in the company. The custodians of the legal obligation to the employees are the EOT's trustees, whose responsibility is simply to determine, annually, that the provisions of the trust are being upheld.

The only US organization that I'm aware of that is involved in the conversion of businesses to both worker cooperatives and EOTs is Project Equity in California. Hilary Abell, the cofounder, said to me, "We are part of the emerging cohort of EOT service providers and enthusiasts. We have completed two EOT transitions to-date. . . . We do find that some owners are more drawn to the EOT than to worker co-ops." It will be interesting to watch Project Equity's next few years because of its broad experience with worker co-ops and this new experience with EOTs. It will also be interesting to find out what is driving companies in each direction.

Two of the big advantages of EOTs over ESOPs are cost and simplicity. EOTs generally cost $50,000 to $100,000 to establish (like worker co-ops), while ESOP start-up costs can range from $150,000 to $500,000. Annual maintenance costs are minimal for EOTs (also like worker co-ops) but can be $30,000 or more for ESOPs.[2] Clearly, ESOPs are appropriate for larger companies, while EOTs and worker co-ops can work for any size company, small or large.

Regarding simplicity, federal regulations require that ESOPs have an annual formal appraisal to determine share value, and they must follow extensive rules and formulas regarding the plan participants. EOTs, however, must only conform with state trust law and follow the bylaws set up by the business owner or the board. This simplicity may not always be an advantage, as we will see.

Mark Hand, at the University of Texas Arlington, and Jenny Everett, a social impact adviser from Austin, publish a lively and informative weekly newsletter called EO+WD (employee ownership and workplace democracy). The two advocate for the EOT model and also cover a wide range of other employee ownership news. In conversation with them, I asked what's responsible for the growing interest in EOTs. Mark thinks it's coming from business owners who "like the purpose piece of the perpetual purpose trust and [are] baking that into the trust structure in an intentional way that allows them to preserve the values and aspects they want to enshrine."

The National Center for Employee Ownership has now recognized EOTs as one of the three major forms of employee ownership. State employee ownership centers have followed suit, and state-by-state legislation to permit EOTs in perpetuity is proceeding as well. According to Mark, along with the Oregon "stewardship trust" legislation mentioned previously, Illinois is creating "virtuous trust" legislation, and various other states have also begun to adjust their statutes to allow for EOTs.[3]

The name "employee ownership trust" can be misleading because the employees don't actually own the business. In search of the right name to distinguish these trusts from other kinds of trusts, advocates have variously suggested calling EOTs "virtuous trusts," "stewardship trusts," "purpose trusts," and "employee-centered trusts." At least for now, "employee ownership trust" is the most commonly used name.

An ecosystem of researchers and practitioners focused on EOTs has begun to emerge in the United States, and more companies are now making the conversion. The first to become an EOT using US trust law (aside from one forerunner in 1897 and another in 1926) was Mētis Construction in Seattle in 2016.

CHRIS MICHAEL

Chris Michael was the earliest promoter of EOTs in the United States. In 2009, he became excited about employee ownership while he was doing a PhD. When he spoke to a few people about his new passion, they suggested that if he really wanted to help grow the field and help businesses convert, a law degree would probably be more valuable than a PhD. "I literally went home that night, bought the [Law School Admission Test] books, and dug in," says Chris.

The trust idea came to him while looking for a better employee ownership mechanism, and he wrote an article about it in 2015. Then, in 2016, while he was scrolling through Twitter, he says, "The whole UK thing unfurled before my eyes and I realized that what I thought I had invented out of whole cloth is called an employee ownership trust, and they've been doing them in the UK for a hundred years."

Chris's firm, EOT Advisors, has led multiple EOT conversions.

When I asked why an EOT is preferable to a worker co-op, Chris had a good answer: "If people want to do a worker co-op, I think the best way to structure it is by using an EOT. If you want to call it a worker cooperative trust, let's do it. I'll pop the champagne on your worker cooperative trust." Mark Hand said something similar when I asked the same question. The reason they say that is because the EOT provides more long-term mission protection than a direct-share worker co-op in which workers are the true owners. "I think these are two different ways to create a worker co-op," says Chris.

This notion interests me. Who wants to be first?

THE JOHN LEWIS PARTNERSHIP

The British EOT concept may have originated with John Spedan Lewis. In 1920, he had a radical idea: that the fifty-six-year-old small business that was handed down to him by his father could be successful and socially responsible at once. Today, the John Lewis Partnership is the United Kingdom's largest employee-owned business, with over seventy-four thousand partners. The sprawling business contains two important retail brands, more than 360 stores, a soft furnishings factory, distribution centers, three cookery schools, a content production hub, a heritage center, and a farm.

Mark Hand told me, "In the United Kingdom, ownership trusts are now almost exclusively used to benefit employees, thanks to legislation in the mid-2010s creating a class of purpose trust-owned companies called employee ownership trusts. After the establishment of generous tax incentives in 2014, EOTs took off in the United Kingdom." In exchange for meeting certain requirements, the owner selling to an EOT pays no capital gains tax on the sale, the employees are eligible for limited tax-free bonuses, and the company gets tax relief for the expense of purchasing EOT shares. The United States has none of these tax benefits for EOTs.

Authors Corey Rosen and John Case write:

In the UK's 2011 Parliamentary elections, leaders of all three major parties at the time pledged to create a *John Lewis economy*. The pledges made front-page news and ultimately led to 2014 legislation creating new rules and benefits for employee ownership trusts.[4]

According to the Employee Ownership Association of the United Kingdom, there were more than 1,650 employee-owned businesses in Great Britain at the end of 2023, and more than 1,300 of those were EOTs.

The John Lewis Partnership expects to preserve the company's employee ownership for current and future generations of employees. The goal is to improve the lives of its workers with significant profit-sharing and a workplace culture that treats every employee with the dignity of a co-owner. In its operation, John Lewis is, again, similar to a worker co-op in terms of wealth-sharing, employee engagement, and distributed management.

Mark Hand and Jenny Everett told me, "The fundamental difference between EOTs in the United States and in Britain is the tax advantages that we don't have [at least not yet]. But those breaks are attached to requirements you must fulfill, so your flexibility is diminished while your benefits are increased."

GRAEME NUTTALL

Several people involved in US EOTs directed me to Graeme Nuttall and indicated that he is the leading UK EOT advocate and expert. Graeme is an attorney who has spent his entire career doing employee ownership policymaking and research in various positions and organizations. The 2014 EOT legislation was largely the result of Graeme's findings about mainstreaming employee ownership of private companies.

Graeme has also been instrumental in supporting the development of the US EOT movement. During an April 2024 interview, he talked about EOTs and their success in Great Britain:

The employee ownership trust model has exceeded expectations and become the UK's default model of employee ownership. The recent runaway success of UK employee ownership, propelled by the EOT, has attracted the attention of other countries, and I am working to develop the EOT and employee ownership internationally.

He made the distinction between direct employee ownership (in which employees own shares, like ESOPs and worker co-ops) and indirect employee ownership (in which a trust owns the shares on behalf of the employees, like EOTs). He said that EOTs have the practical advantage of "fewer moving parts."

Is this an advantage? One of the missing moving parts is the protections for employee-owners that ERISA (the Employee Retirement Income Security Act) in the United States provides for ESOPs and that worker governance rights provide for worker co-ops.

Graeme has a lofty ambition: he would ultimately like to see an internationally shared understanding that a trust is an EOT "when its purpose is to provide permanent or long-term employee ownership of a company, through holding a significant proportion of a company's shares on trust for the benefit of all the company's employees."

Consistent with his ambitions regarding standardization, Graeme would prefer that American EOTs continue to be called EOTs, assuming that they do what they say and provide what he calls "long-term employee ownership" that delivers profit-sharing, employee engagement, and other elements of good work.

It doesn't sound like he'll stop pushing for that shared understanding anytime soon, and his successes to date suggest that it may not be too much of a reach.

EOT SKEPTICISM

Despite all the enthusiasm, there are EOT skeptics. The doubts are essentially about two things: the fact that EOTs do not confer actual ownership to employees and a concern that, given the newness of the approach, we have not encountered the inevitable unintended consequences or fully wrestled with the technical complications inherent to the structure.

Alex Moss of Praxis says, "I have a slightly cynical view. EOTs do not have the inherent worker protections that ESOPs and co-ops do, and they don't build equity value for workers. My real concern with EOTs is that if you want to change wealth inequality, you have to actually give people the opportunity to build wealth."

Allison Curtis of the ICA Group says, "The trust falls closer to stewardship than actual ownership in which employees are given a voice in the entire direction of the firm."

Matthias Scheiblehner is the founder of Mētis Construction in Seattle. In 2016, Mētis was the first modern EOT in the United States to be established using US trust law. Chris Michael was the legal consultant who helped Matthias and his colleagues to make this happen. Matthias has since left the company and has a new construction company in Missoula, Montana, called Rhizome. He expects to convert that company to an EOT, too, once he has its feet firmly planted.

Matthias is a strong advocate of democratic EOTs. When he was invited to be on the board of a newly formed EOT and read through the trust agreement, he saw nothing about democratic governance, participatory management, or employee engagement. The board of trustees decides the benefits for the workers. "It's like, we're going to take good care of you," says Matthias. "That's not what people want. I think we need an architecture that assures employees of a significant voice and includes a board of trustees made up of employees. An EOT is only as democratic as the language on which it is founded."

This speaks to the concern that EOTs can be highly beneficial for employees, but they aren't necessarily so. Employee rights are not an EOT structural requirement as they are in a worker co-op.

Jason Wiener, the attorney we met in chapter 4 who has been instrumental in the Colorado worker ownership movement, says, "I'm an open-minded skeptic of the purpose trust, to the extent that it's being marketed and sold as nearly a universal solution, and I think that's problematic for a few reasons. One, there's no preferential tax treatment whatsoever for an ownership trust. It does not qualify for 1042 rollover like ESOPs and worker co-ops can." (The 1042 rollover is an Internal Revenue Service provision that allows selling owners of ESOPs and worker co-ops who meet certain requirements to defer capital gains tax on sale proceeds.)

He continues:

The big thing is, I think it's misnamed. It is not an employee *ownership* trust. It is administered by a disinterested trustee and does not necessarily or inherently empower employees or give them voice, although some EOTs add this feature through trust protector committees. I think we may find that direct workplace democracy and trustee-led purpose will be at odds. I am more skeptical of the ability of a disinterested trustee's ability to carry out a company's mission to advance employees' interest than employees' ability to navigate these same issues and decide themselves what's best for them and future generations of workers. That said, I have recommended and built purpose trusts for clients, and I do believe they belong in the toolkit, just in limited applications.

I doubt we will know the degree of truth in these concerns for some time, as more EOTs form and more history and experience accumulate. EOT advocates feel that these are the early days, a period of experimentation, and we will solve these potential problems over time.

COMMON TRUST

Derek Razo has no doubts. Quite the opposite. He is the cofounder and one of the two managing partners of Common Trust (Zoe Schlag is the other). Common Trust is responsible for roughly a third of the US EOTs formed to date.

Although Derek is a strong and articulate EOT advocate, in no way does he feel that he has all the answers. He agrees about the early-stage experimentation. He said to me in April 2024:

> I think right now there's a battle for the soul of the EOT movement, and the battle is between people who want it to be a specific kind of thing and are willing to use regulation and policy and institutional legitimacy to try to force the sector to become a certain thing. And there's a group of people who are truly trying to discover what the thing is and what it wants to be. I'm firmly in the second group, trying to discover what's right in each case, implementing that, and assuming when there's a critical mass of EOTs in place we can go back and assess what's working and what's not. Let's grow the space in an unconstrained petri dish and look back empirically.

The point, he says, is to recognize what people really care about. It's the ability to benefit from the surplus fruits of your labor and have a protected way to have a voice in the destiny of your work. People care about the operational realities, not the structure.

Derek paints a picture of an iterative collaborative project among people who have been developing this approach in their own ways. He points out that the biggest contributors of all have been *the business owners themselves*—they are leading the way. He considers them to be deeply insightful people for whom the conversion to an EOT (or other form of employee ownership) is not even the most important thing they've done. They have spent twenty to thirty years, with boots on the ground, building a culture worth preserving. The EOT is just the mechanism for accomplishing the preservation.

"So that's my main message," Derek says. "The businesses are the most important contributors. It's their thing. They're the reason it exists—not us."

His words resonate with me, a former business owner who did an employee ownership conversion and lived it for decades. The more that each ownership and management approach can be designed and built so that it serves the owner's dreams and the employees' desires at once, the greater success we'll see.

Text-Em-All is a good example.

TEXT-EM-ALL

Sometimes you meet a business owner who is overflowing with enthusiasm and seems to have all the wood behind a single arrow pointed in the right direction. Brad Herrmann, the owner of software company Text-Em-All, is like that. I had a long conversation with him in April 2024.

After finishing business school at Texas A&M, he worked at Andersen Consulting for a few years, where he learned programming. He then joined the engineering team in his father's software company, Ti3, from 1997 to 2005. It wasn't until the company was sold to a much larger publicly owned company in 2001 that Brad began to realize how good he had it in previous years. With the sale of the company, it began to turn into something quite different.

Hai Nguyen came to Ti3 in 2001, and Brad and Hai ran it together after Brad's father retired. But—after the sale—Brad and Hai had a different kind of boss. "We couldn't keep corporate from messing with our successful little division down here in Texas," Brad told me. "Suddenly we had decisions coming down from the top. You weren't supposed to question them—just shut up and do it. I thought it was about the bigness, but I learned that it's not that I can't do big. It's that I can't do shitty culture."

It turns out that Brad's father had been very good at building healthy organizational culture. They didn't call it that back then—it was just a cool place to work, with shared financials and profit-sharing. Ask anything, challenge anything, have fun together. Brad loved it.

But when Hai and Brad lost the parts of their work that they loved, Brad knew he needed to start a new business. He worked on a business plan, got a commitment from his dad and another family member to invest, went to Hai, and said, "Hey, I'm going to leave and start my own thing, and I'd love to have you do it with me. He was like, 'Oh, you and your dad? I'm in. All the way.'"

The business is a communication platform primarily used for sending mass messages and voice broadcasts for emergency notifications, event reminders, appointment confirmations, and fundraising campaigns. It can be particularly beneficial for health care, education, nonprofits, religious organizations, and businesses that require efficient and reliable communication with clients and employees.

When they began, smartphone texting was just coming of age. They went into it with an unusual mindset: make the product work, turn a profit, make a "badass workplace" where everyone likes to be, and use the products for good purpose. They were not interested in making a company to sell; they wanted to make a hundred-year company to keep. Live life and enjoy it!

This is a software and service company, the epitome of the modern economy, and the goal is supposed to be to make it valuable, sell it to private equity, and ride off into the billionaire sunset. Right?

Not for Hai and Brad. Why ride anywhere? They want to stay put and keep the company private. They built a strong business and culture, something worth sustaining and protecting, with a very engaged team. Brad says, "People tell me all the time that working here has been a life-changing event. 'I'm never leaving—you'll have to throw me out.'"

I asked how they got interested in employee ownership.

"I feel passionately that people show up here every day and bust their butt and deserve to get part of the wealth they help to generate," Brad said. "But we couldn't find an obvious solution. We looked hard at ESOPs—in fact, we got very close to enacting an ESOP and found some hidden complications that our attorney hadn't revealed. Bailed right out and haven't talked to him since."

They never thought to look at the worker co-op. Fortunately, they were exposed to the EOT and talked to a few people in that world, but they still didn't quite find what they were looking for. It was too complicated—or at least it seemed so at first. "We love and value simplicity," Brad said. "We're very lean, maybe too lean sometimes."

Then they ran into Common Trust. According to Brad:

We knew we had the right thing when they asked, on the first call, "What is it about your company that you want to protect and make perpetual? What's your purpose? Can you put that into words?" This was about something bigger, and immediately it was like, bam, that's it. Nobody else had led with that question. And we never looked back. What was also great about Common Trust is that they handled everything in-house. It was just a direct collaboration between us and them. Simple.

Text-Em-All became an employee ownership trust on October 1, 2023. When we spoke, the company had issued two quarterly profit shares. Brad said, "It's not like we didn't have a wonderful mindset already. We went from a ten to an eleven. But people do say that folks are acting differently now, with a stronger sense of ownership."

There you have it. Do the work. Build a great company. Then make an even-greater company with proscribed employee benefits and share the wealth. For the next hundred years.

Sounds pretty good to me. Like I've said before, it's not the model that matters; it's the case-by-case manifestation of the chosen model that does.

We've now examined the three major forms of employee ownership. I wonder what you're thinking right now. I wonder if you're finding yourself more attracted to the worker co-op or the ESOP or the EOT. Or if you have more questions now than you did when you started. I hope some will be answered in Part Three of the book.

But wait, there are more options.

CHAPTER 8

NEW INNOVATIONS, OUTLIERS, AND PRIVATE EQUITY

Along with worker co-ops, employee stock ownership plans (ESOPs), and employee ownership trusts (EOTs), a variety of newer alternative ownership approaches are developing. Some of these deserve caution for now, some don't, and all deserve consideration. The result of this innovation and experimentation may be to add strength, breadth, and vitality to the quest to make employee ownership widespread.

The alternative that provokes the most questions is private equity as it wades into the employee ownership sphere. But first, let's look at other new options.

DIRECT STOCK OWNERSHIP

To explain how direct stock ownership works and why it's worthy of consideration, I share this story of an advocate and his endeavors.

In 1988, Chip Cargas was forty-one years old. After a career in engineering and another in human resources, he was ready to start his own business. He named it Cargas, and at first it was a one-person consulting firm located in the corner of a bedroom. When I spoke with Chip in May 2024, Cargas had become a company with two hundred employees providing software solutions for business.

Open-book finance and deep collaboration were company hallmarks from the beginning. Eight years in, Chip started an egalitarian profit-sharing plan.

Everyone participates. Profit-sharing is determined half by years of service and the other half is one share per person.

At a local chamber of commerce meeting in his area (Lancaster, Pennsylvania), Chip heard a speaker talk about his hundred-person company that practiced direct share ownership (DSO)—the employees own stock in the company. He said to himself, "This is the final piece of the puzzle to flesh out my founding desire to all be in this together and share the wealth we create."

Today, a stock offer comes with each Cargas job offer.

There's a proscribed amount of stock an employee can buy; the amount increases over time. To buy more, you need to be "a key driver of success," as Chip puts it. In most cases, that's a top leader, but not always—it can be any individual contributor who's making a big impact. Eight employees have now accumulated more than a million dollars' worth of stock, and more than twenty others have over a hundred thousand, with many others on similar trajectories.

"Why would a DSO be, for owners, preferable to other forms of employee ownership?" I asked Chip.

"Take my case," he responded. "I was a 100 percent owner for ten years. When we first provided the opportunity for others to buy stock, I was 99 percent owner, and a few people had tiny slices. It progressed over time, and now, after twenty-six years, I'm down to 2 percent. During that time, the second generation of leaders took on more responsibility as they bought more stock. Emotionally, it would have been hard for me to sell 30 percent or 50 percent or 100 percent of the company all at once. I felt that if we eased into it, there would be no damage done if it didn't work. It was easier for me to wrap my head around it this way."

A new CEO is now in place after a deliberate transition process, Chip has very few remaining responsibilities, and during 2025 he plans to be fully retired. But Chip has a new plan to build on the Cargas success.

As he explains, "So here I am, seventy-five years old, nearly retired, with a bit of energy and brain power left, so what can I do? I decided to tell the story of DSO and spread the word, and I formed Tandem to do it."

The Tandem Center for Shared Business Success is a nonprofit dedicated to educating and providing technical assistance about direct share ownership, profit-sharing, and collaborative management. Chip launched it in partnership with the Lancaster Chamber of Commerce, the Pennsylvania Center for Employee Ownership (PaCEO), and the National Center for Employee Ownership (NCEO). Their plan is to start locally by testing and developing their ideas in Lancaster County.

All of this seems positive, but it leaves me with questions. It may be less egalitarian than it appears. When Chip says that to buy more stock than proscribed you must be identified as "a key driver of success," someone must be making that determination; there is a top-down aspect. And although it sounds like employee engagement is commendably high, I did not get a sense that the employees have governance rights. It's different to be "given" a voice than to be ensured of one.

Loren Rodgers, the executive director of NCEO, who has broad experience with all forms of employee ownership, accepted a position on the Tandem board of directors. I asked him what makes NCEO bullish enough on DSO that he would join their board, and what he sees as DSO advantages over other forms of employee ownership.

NCEO is an advocate, he said, because of "the general principle that employee ownership is best served when there are many mechanisms to create it, so we fill as many niches as we can." He adds that "DSO has some fuzzy lines. There's not a sharp definition yet, but I expect one will emerge, and I expect it'll include some requirements for broad participation in ownership and formulaic participation, as you suggest, rather than discretionary merit-based wealth building."

His point is well taken. The more options, the broader the appeal can be. But Loren suggests that the vague aspects of this model need to be specified in greater detail. And other questions remain: How does the DSO company create a market for its stock? How do employees redeem their holdings? Until the model is clarified and the questions are answered, direct stock ownership does not yet, in my view, qualify as broad-based employee ownership.

Maybe it will, in time. Meanwhile, the work Chip and Tandem are doing is important, and Cargas shares more than (probably) 99 percent of the companies in the world.

WORKER COOPERATIVE HOLDING COMPANIES

A worker cooperative holding company is a hybrid of a worker co-op and a corporate holding company. Subsidiary companies are owned wholly or in part by a central entity. These companies are managed partly at the cooperative holding company level and partly by workers at the subsidiary level, in differing degrees.

There are not many cooperative holding companies. I know of only three in the United States operating at present: Evergreen Cooperatives in Cleveland, Obran Cooperative in Seattle, and Spokane Workers Cooperative in eastern Washington State. Each has a different structure. Evergreen is a nonprofit corporation, Obran is a cooperative conglomerate, and Spokane is a limited cooperative association. All have the potential and the aspiration to grow, but it's too soon to know whether they will successfully grow the model in the long term and spread significant wealth to workers.

Empowered Ventures, the thriving ESOP holding company discussed in chapter 6, is an example of an employee ownership holding company of a different sort.

There may be others.

Evergreen Cooperatives

Evergreen Cooperatives is the oldest and most proven of the three cooperative holding companies that I highlight here. In 2008, representatives of the Cleveland Foundation, the City of Cleveland, the Democracy Collaborative, and the Ohio Employee Ownership Center convened a roundtable with the CEOs of three key Cleveland "anchor institutions"—Case Western Reserve University, the Cleveland Clinic, and University Hospitals. The group decided to try to revitalize low-to-medium income neighborhoods through employee ownership.

The strategy they developed was for the nonprofit Evergreen to acquire small and mid-sized businesses, convert them to worker cooperatives, and provide training, business support, and oversight to help them become robust companies. Evergreen owns 20 percent of each company; the workers own the rest.

I spoke to Evergreen's CEO John McMicken. Evergreen has five operating worker co-ops, each with their own governance and business operations: Evergreen Cooperative Laundry (which serves local hospitals), Berry Insulation (which provides insulation and weatherization services), Phoenix Coffee (a wholesale coffee roaster and commissary bakery, with six coffeeshops), Intellitronix (a producer of LED automotive aftermarket digital and analog gauges), and Lefco Worthington (a manufacturer of engineered custom wood crates and heavy-duty skids for shipping). The nonprofit Evergreen also operates two subsidiaries: Evergreen Business Services (a back-office support team) and the Fund for Cooperative Development (a revolving loan fund that does the acquisitions and co-op conversions).

All seven entities are in the Cleveland area. When I spoke to John, there were 320 total employees, and revenues were approaching $30 million (up from $3 million in 2013, when John was hired). The businesses cannot be sold or demutualized without the approval of the nonprofit.

After many challenges in the early days, John feels that the model is working well. They began distributing meaningful profits in 2017, and in 2023, the yearly average profit distribution was just under $10,000 per employee-owner. This is having impact: "We see home ownership on the rise," John said. "You see more and more nice cars in the parking lot. These things are game-changing."

He notes that the commercial laundry model has significant potential and "is attractive to many larger health care systems who would love to have their laundry done locally but often don't have the option—because most laundry providers are in rural areas where land and labor is cheap. Some hospitals are understanding that value would come from paying a bit more for their laundry processing to have it done literally down the street, in the neighborhoods they serve."

Evergreen is now active in nearby Columbus, and the five-year plan is to look at other markets. This is a successful and well-integrated model that is sure to expand its reach. Others have tried to emulate it, and I suspect that will continue.

Obran Cooperative

Obran is a cooperative conglomerate that emphasizes underserved workers. Their website explains: "Founded in 2019 by a group of returning citizens in Baltimore City, Obran's work is built to center those closest to the problem of economic and social oppression."[1]

Hendrix Berry, the chief compliance officer at Obran Capital, explained that "we convert businesses to worker ownership through acquisition, by finding businesses that are for sale and subsuming them into our one worker cooperative, rather than spinning off individual worker cooperatives."

Workers in the subsidiary businesses ultimately own and control at least 51 percent of the holding company. The employees of the held companies become employees of the holding company cooperative, where business services, such as payroll, bookkeeping, accounting, legal, human resources, and acquisition are centralized. Four of the five board members are elected by the employee-owners, and one is an investor.

When I spoke to Hendrix in May 2024, there were five businesses under the Obran umbrella, and negotiations were under way with several others. The combined businesses have over 450 employees and approximately 135 employee-owners. The barriers to becoming a worker-owner are extremely low—a ninety-day waiting period and $250 membership fee—but the current benefits are hard to explain to employees because they are not (yet) able to share wealth. As a worker-owner, you get to own the company that owns your business, but time will tell what that really means.

Obran passed the threshold of profitability in 2023, and it expects to distribute dividends in 2025. About twenty of the employee-owners work in the holding company, providing services to the held companies and acting as the motor that drives Obran forward. The remainder work in the held companies.

Carolyn Edsell-Vetter of the Cooperative Fund of the Northeast (CFNE) says, "Obran's social mission is still relatively unique among worker-owned firms: centering building power and wealth for workers of color, including formerly incarcerated workers. The majority of employee-owned firms were formerly led by white men, and white men have made up the majority of the new owners created by new transitions. Obran is one of the few approaches working to interrupt this 'success to the successful' dynamic that continues to concentrate power and wealth among one class of people."

The authors of *Assets in Common* add that "Obran is an effort to create a worker cooperative that benefits from the same economies of scale enjoyed by large corporations but for the benefit of working-class employees. Doing so is fairly uncharted territory, and as trailblazers, Obran is likely to get some thorns and scratches along the way."[2]

The aspirations are admirable, and it will be interesting to follow Obran's progress in the years to come to see how successful it can be and whether it inspires others. Already, I have spoken to one individual who is working to assemble an enterprise to follow in Obran's footsteps.

Spokane Workers Cooperative

Joel Williamson grew up in Spokane, working for his father on the flower farm that was started by his great grandfather in 1917. When the farm folded in 1998, he went to school to pursue his theater interests and toured (doing the lighting) with a play written by three contemporaries. The play shared their experiences as people of color in this country. That awakened his political and economic consciousness ("Good art does that," he said to me), and he began to question the nature of change. He saw how his new thinking resonated with what he had learned in the family business.

Back in Spokane, Joel looked for ways to be a force for good in his community. When he stumbled on the co-op model and then learned about the flower growers' cooperative his great-grandfather started in the 1930s, he was drawn back to business. Eastern Washington is wheat country, and he saw that local brewers needed locally produced malt. He and a friend with a similar family farming background started LINK foods as both a producer co-op and a worker co-op. Later, they started the Grain Shed, which used the local ingredients produced by LINK to make bread and beer and operate a restaurant.

At that point, he met Luke Baumgartner, another "Spokie" who owned and operated several businesses in town. They joined forces. Inspired by Obran, they established the Spokane Workers Cooperative (SWC) to preserve local businesses that were facing the departure of their founders. SWC used the help of angel investors and cooperative financing nonprofits, like Seed Commons, to acquire five local businesses.

They learned how hard it is to build ownership culture in businesses unfamiliar with the co-op approach. Now, they have halted acquisitions temporarily as they work to help their existing businesses thrive and gain employee engagement. Joel devotes a significant part of his time to growing LINK and the Grain

Shed while still maintaining his ties to SWC. He thinks they will ultimately get back to business acquisitions as they learn how to identify the kinds of businesses that will work best in their system. Joel's a committed, dyed-in-the-wool co-op person, working in several arenas to make co-ops work and scale.

Obran and Spokane are new models that deserve attention and observation. Employee ownership organizations and developers are intrigued by the potential, but the jury is still out. These models have yet to generate the wealth or traction to prove that they can successfully spread employee ownership and wealth and become an important succession path for small businesses. Evergreen, however, appears to have a mature working model with potential to influence, grow, and spread.

PRIVATE EQUITY

Private equity, which the Democracy Collaborative's Marjorie Kelly describes as the apex predator in our economy, has a significant new interest in employee ownership. That interest grabs our attention and merits serious consideration, with eyes wide open.

In general, private equity has a voracious appetite for the acquisition of successful small businesses, and rules do not appear to apply. Journalist Rachel Phua, writing in the *American Prospect*, says:

> Private equity busts unions, violates labor laws, puts workers safety at risk, removes companies from communities, disrupts good jobs, and often dismantles and sells companies for parts. The largest source of private equity funding comes from public pensions. This means that workers are funding all this bad behavior that has direct negative impact on their lives.[3]

The private equity threat is one reason why mission-driven companies must be deliberate and intentional about succession plans and mission protection. When you wish to sell your business hoping the good work you have begun can continue, the ready buyer with plenty of cash may have other plans, with tragic consequences. Many small business owners have seen friends sell their businesses to private equity only to end up with fat wallets and broken hearts.

Private equity (PE) typically requires both ownership and control. Once a company is owned and run by investors, its path changes. The PE end game is to sell the company for big returns without concern for what becomes of it. Any company owner intending to protect long-term mission must beware.

Most private equity ownership deals do not involve the small businesses this book is about. For that reason, my treatment of the subject will be limited, except for a few outlier examples of new models that appear to have great potential. The best current in-depth resource I've found about this subject is a 2024 paper by NCEO's Corey Rosen called "Private Equity and Employee Ownership."

Kohlberg, Kravis, and Roberts

The PE firm that has gotten the most attention regarding employee ownership (including a segment on *60 Minutes*) is the notorious Kohlbeg, Kravis, and Roberts (KKR). Yes, this is the infamous firm in the 1980s book and film *Barbarians at the Gate.*

Pete Stavros is a KKR partner and is co-head of Global Private Equity. In addition, he is the founder and major funder of a nonprofit called Ownership Works, which advocates and trains executives to implement the KKR model of employee ownership into their businesses.[4] Stavros has emerged as the leading PE advocate for employee ownership. Using the model he created, KKR had brought forty-seven companies with one hundred thousand employees into "employee ownership" by mid-2024.

In a 2024 episode of *60 Minutes,* commentator Jon Wertheim says of Stavros, "He criss-crosses the country preaching his gospel at business schools and before DC lawmakers, advocating to update the tax code to incentivize employee ownership, which he hopes will soon be standard business practice, not an exotic exception."[5]

As Stavros makes his pitch, he speaks the language of employee ownership and conveys valuable sentiments. He says that there is too much wealth inequality (but reluctantly admits that KKR's work makes it worse), and he says that workers need hope—they need to share a piece of the pie and a voice in their work. "Day one, we sit down with the workforce," he says. "We explain at a very high level, 'This is our business plan. This is where we're headed. These are the key priorities. There is a pool of ownership set aside for you.'"[6]

Stavros goes on to say that it is crucial for employees to feel a sense of ownership over the products or services they are manufacturing for customers. If employees consciously know that they are an important part of the company, they will personally invest in producing products of the highest quality.

Since this message makes employees feel like they belong, they work harder, the company makes more money, and then the PE firm sells the company five or seven years later for more than it otherwise would have. The sale enriches the employee-owners (a little) and enriches the company owners (a lot). A small piece of the pie placates the workers, jobs may disappear, and private equity continues to fill its coffers. Is this better than if PE steered clear of employee ownership entirely? It's hard to say.

Corey Rosen quotes Pulitzer-prize winning journalist Gretchen Morgenson in his recent paper:

> KKR brags that its recent sale of CHI Doors resulted in employees getting an average of $175,000 each, but the sale was for a whopping $3 billion, netting KKR itself a staggering 10-fold return on its original investment after including dividends paid to it. More recently, KKR sold GeoStabilization, giving employees an average of $83,000 each before taxes. The best estimates are that KKR investors saw a return of $1.1 billion. As one employee said, "I'm gonna buy a new car!" This is not employee ownership. This is Kool-Aid for the workers. ESOPs are designed to create a real future for working people. These deceptive practices by PE serve to exacerbate the wage and wealth gap, exactly what employee ownership was designed to remedy. Many in the business and employee ownership worlds argue that "at least the employees get something." That is a straw horse and is equivalent to saying, "At least those in poverty get food stamps."[7]

Deep skepticism is warranted. Private equity firms still appear to be wolves, even in their new sheep's clothing.

Two Guitar Companies

Speaking of sheep and wolves, let's look at the contrasting stories of Taylor Guitars and Gibson Guitars.[8]

The founding owners of Taylor Guitars sold 100 percent of the company, with its 1,200 employees and $122 million in annual revenues, to an ESOP trust.

The purchase was financed by Social Capital Trust, a Canadian pension fund. The debt has favorable terms. Once the loan is paid off, the workers will own the firm free and clear and enjoy the full potential of the financial upside.

Gibson Guitars, on the other hand, was purchased by KKR in 2018. After piling on new debt to give a special $225 million dividend to its private equity partners, it announced a $7 million profit share for Gibson's eight hundred workers. That is a one-time payment of about $9,000 each (less than the amount of profit-sharing and dividends that little South Mountain Company shares *each year*). The employees will probably receive something more when the company is inevitably sold, but that sale is likely to result in downsizing, layoffs, and all the other damaging moves that characterize private equity's model.

In some cases, employees receive life-changing payouts, but this is the exception, not the rule. Essentially, this type of private equity management uses employee ownership to further enrich the 1 percent.

Nick Romeo writes in *The Alternative*, "Using a single umbrella term like *worker ownership* to refer to drastically different levels of ownership is imprecise at best. At worst, it allows predatory private equity firms to co-opt the worker-ownership movement, claiming to share its goals without implementing its content: that workers own their companies and actively govern them."[9]

Jason Wiener, the Colorado employee ownership attorney, said to me, "Unless you can show me incentives that don't lead to liquidity events, I am skeptical that you can achieve greater wealth, power, and income for workers' bottom line. That's the thing I think is so simple about a worker co-op. It is built not to liquidate."

Blackstone, the biggest private equity giant of all, has now jumped into employee ownership. I doubt it will be any different from KKR's approach. It's a great thing that there will be additional wealth distribution (although the numbers are tiny), but the heading-for-a-sale mentality that drives private equity makes it less appealing. The big dogs entering employee ownership is like greenwashing. We might call it wealthwashing.

Abe Lincoln and Eric Rieger

There's a story about Abraham Lincoln, when he was still practicing law in Springfield, Illinois. It may be apocryphal, or it may be true; I can't tell.

As the story goes, Lincoln represented a client who was fighting the railroad. A friend approaching Lincoln's office saw a man come flying out the door, with Lincoln behind him shaking his fist. The friend rushed in to see what had happened.

"I threw him out," Lincoln said.

"Why? What did he do?" asked the friend.

"He's the lawyer for the railroad, and he offered me $5,000 to betray my client, but I turned him down. Then he offered me $10,000, and I turned him down again, and finally he offered me $15,000 and I threw him out." The friend asked why he had chosen that moment to throw him out.

"Because," Lincoln answered, "he was getting close to my price."

The lure of the single-minded pursuit of financial success is strong. Sometimes it comes close to our price. Lincoln, as we know, had no price.

That's the case for many business owners, too. Like Eric Rieger, owner of a successful technology company in the Chicago suburbs called WEBIT Services, who has received multiple acquisition offers. He is figuring out which employee ownership model is best for his company because he saw what happened to several friends who sold companies to private equity. They "took their seven figure paychecks and, to a person, they're all miserable. They sold their souls, and their employees got the shaft." He said to me that he'll never sell, except to his employees.

But let's look at several versions of private equity and PE-like innovations that may prove to be more beneficial and perhaps highly impactful in positive ways.

Teamshares

One organization that may be trying to use private equity in a fundamentally different way is called Teamshares, which buys small businesses from retiring owners. At the closing, it grants 10 percent ownership of the business's stock to employees, and it intends to progressively increase employee ownership to 80 percent within twenty years. Employees earn stock through ongoing service. They do not have to buy it.

Teamshares has quietly raised $245 million in venture capital, which it uses to buy small profitable companies from retiring owners in blue-collar, recession-proof industries with long-standing loyal employees—like butcher shops, paint stores, auto repair shops, small manufacturers, and home improvement contractors—mostly very small businesses. More than ninety businesses in thirty-one states were purchased in the company's first five years. Many of the owners had no succession plans, no other buyer prospects, and no idea how to sustain their creations beyond their tenures, until Teamshares came along.

Teamshares has big plans, including the development of services like banking, insurance, and health care plans to sell to and service their business network. The vision is to create a system of financially durable companies with retiring owners and new employee-owners who are all better off. "These companies will never be for sale again, a win for employee-owners and for local economies," said Michael Brown, the cofounder and chief executive of Teamshares.[10]

Corey Rosen says:

> To date, no one has tried to purchase a disparate group of companies in sectors that traditionally have low profitability and high turnover in a way that can provide the kind of return that . . . outside investors expect. Part of the success of Teamshares will . . . hinge on whether the shared services model proves to be one that can generate long-term profitability for Teamshares and reduce costs for the companies that it is purchasing. It is also too soon to assess whether the shares employees will receive will accrue significant value and if the companies will be able to have the liquidity to repurchase.[11]

It's also too soon to know if they can really achieve 80 percent employee ownership. Twenty years is a long time. Will they never be sold again? Many in the employee ownership arena are doubtful. Teamshares may have a different goal than most private equity firms, but the funding is still from private equity, and private equity rarely forgoes big returns. But for now, at least, some companies that had no discernible path forward have found one by joining this endeavor.

Dave Hammer of ICA explains as follows:

> What Teamshares does, which is fascinating, is that for every single project, they hire someone from the outside to come in and take over that company after the founder departs. You could critique that. But what

they're also doing is building cohorts of those presidents who go through training together. That's exactly the kind of thing that cooperatives should and could be doing.

Teamshares is requiring that these companies buy services from them, but these services should make the companies more effective, and they put managers in to ensure profitability. If Teamshares holds true to its twenty-year goals, there could be a positive outcome. Hammer continues:

> As soon as I heard about Teamshares, I became interested, as I'm curious about the potential for employee ownership conglomerates. My biggest critique of the approach is that it doesn't give the worker-owners at the individual business the autonomy to make the most important decisions, which would be for the business to do something different, for example. You have less self-determination in a conglomerate, and self-determination is an important part, I think, of freedom and dignity.

Blake Jones said to me, "They are doing these buyouts of companies that are thrilled to have anybody be interested in them at all. That's good. What we don't know is whether it will prove to be what they say it is."

Only time will tell.

APIS & HERITAGE

I close this chapter on an unequivocally positive note with Apis & Heritage Capital Partners (A&H), which is neither a worker cooperative holding company nor private equity. It's something in between that's unlike anything else I've found, with the possible exception of Empowered Ventures, the ESOP holding company. A&H is an investment fund that aims to close the racial wealth gap using employee ownership. The firm raised more than $58 million from impact investors and uses this capital to buy businesses with substantial numbers of low-income workers and workers of color. A&H converts these businesses to ESOPs to try to build new wealth among those often excluded from economic opportunity.

Michael Brownrigg is a cofounder and senior managing director. He calls himself "the old white guy in a company run primarily by younger people of color" (which includes Todd Leverette and Phil Reeves, the other two founders and managing partners). I spoke with Brownrigg at length in June 2024. At the time, A&H had acquired four companies with a combined 375 employees and revenues approaching $60 million. He expected them to close on three more companies in 2024, which would add two hundred more employees.

When A&H purchases these companies, the departing owner is required to finance 10 percent of the purchase price (to have some skin in the game during the early years and to incentivize the founder's help with the leadership transition that will occur). A&H is generally able to get bank financing for another 30 percent and then supplies the remaining 60 percent itself. This is called "mezzanine debt," in acquisition parlance (the debt that fills the gap between owner financing and bank financing), and it comes at a significantly higher rate than bank financing. But it can remove a barrier to ESOP conversions, which is that often the seller must carry that additional 60 percent note.

The result is that, on day one, the departing owner receives 90 percent of the purchase price and the employees own all the shares in the company, which are held in a trust for them. The employees earn additional shares each year they work, and the shares are bought back from them when they retire or depart. Everyone who is helping to build value eventually shares in the wealth created.

A&H charges 13 percent interest, with the funds to pay this coming from future profits of the acquired companies. Most of the interest income goes back to the investors, and some goes to A&H to finance its operations. The theory is that since the companies pay no taxes (having become 100 percent ESOPs) and no longer have an owner who's taking out the surplus profits every year, they will become significantly more profitable and pay off the A&H debt (or much of it) in the first five years. At that point, whatever expensive mezzanine debt remains can be replaced by cheaper bank financing, and the employee-owners' share value, which is low at the time of purchase, will begin to accelerate.

"A&H," says Brownrigg, "exists to make these companies successful so that they can in turn make low-income workers and workers of color wealthier over time. We will do whatever we can to make sure that happens." The A&H role at the time of purchase is to be involved in hiring a new CEO, creating a five-person board (consisting at inception of two members from A&H, one from outside selected by A&H, the new CEO, and one worker rep selected by the employees), and building the systems and ownership culture to create employee engagement and proficiency. This development work is intended to be ongoing, and it is led by the Democracy at Work Institute (DAWI), which has an impeccable reputation in the employee ownership world.

Todd Leverette, who laid the groundwork for A&H while he was working at DAWI, told me in an email that "A&H has its roots in the worker co-op world, and we bring the worker-centeredness and worker voice into our portfolio companies in partnership with [DAWI]."

I spoke to Melissa Hoover, the special projects director at DAWI. She was involved in the founding of both the US Federation of Worker Cooperatives and DAWI and has been a longtime worker co-op leader and voice for expanding the model to underserved populations. She stepped down as DAWI executive director to work with Todd and the others to establish A&H.

The genesis came about when she and Todd realized that capital wasn't being used as a driver for employee ownership conversions. "We workshopped a prototype, a way that you could use a fund to buy businesses and convert them to employee ownership," she says. "Todd brought in his friend Phil Reeves, who has small business experience. They developed the concept further, and they pitched it to me. They came to our New York offices, brought bagels, sat me down and did a proper pitch. I was sold, even though it was a significant step outside the usual boundaries of DAWI's work. I said, 'Let's do it' and I raised money from the Kellogg Foundation and others to fund the incubation work."

Brownrigg entered a bit later and brought his longtime experience raising capital investment. He filled out the team, and they went to work to raise the first round of capital.

Melissa and her team are responsible for building the systems and ownership culture to foster healthy and successful employee-owned companies. She says there is some question in the worker ownership world about DAWI's involvement in capital and ESOPs and how far the organization can stray from pure cooperative forms and still keep their values front and center. She feels that it's worthwhile to push the envelope to tackle the full range of what's possible:

The A&H model is most importantly about democratizing *ownership* of the workplace, and it achieves that from day one. Building [a] worker-centered culture takes longer and takes many forms, but ulti-mately the goal is to end up with a perpetually employee-owned business with structures that support employee voice. I think these are the tools we need to address the racial gap and elevate low-wage jobs. A&H is changing the conversation at a level and in a place where the ripple effects could be enormous.

A&H designates its companies "Esoperatives" and aims for boards com-prised of a majority of employees by the time they exit.

I asked Michael Brownrigg whether their investors can really be considered "impact investors" when they are getting such a high rate of return (not dissimi-lar from the rates that private equity investors receive). His answer was an em-phatic yes. That's "because they backed an unproven team with an untried investment thesis whose aim is to, yes, earn fair risk-adjusted returns while as-suring that business assets transfer into ownership and benefits for low-income workers and workers of color."

One essential difference between A&H and private equity is that, like Em-powered Ventures, A&H is not preparing these businesses for future short-term sales; on the contrary, as Melissa says, they are preparing them for long-term employee ownership and wealth-sharing. A&H has an explicit strategy to con-vert businesses to employee ownership in five to seven years, not twenty, and they are willing to do the work to help employees get to that point. A&H has the potential, in my view, to be the true realization of employee ownership excel-lence and impact using private equity funds, just as ReVision is the true realiza-tion of the potential of the ESOP model.

Like Derek Razo at Common Trust when he talks about EOT experimenta-tion (see chapter 7), Melissa says, "This is a laboratory. We are in a time of intense experimentation, and I think we should support that in every way we can. We are not going to change the economy on the purity of a few small models, but we're also not going to change it with a denatured gestural approach, either. The hope is that we can find the right balance—retain mission and purpose and share wealth while creating something that has the muscle to effect major change."

Alex Moss of Praxis calls it "a PE-like firm with good values. It's who they are doing it for that's impressive. I love the focus and the intent. To my eye, the jury is out on the impact and whether these deals are unnecessarily complex and costly."

Colorado attorney Jason Wiener likes the idea of developing enterprise structures like Teamshares and A&H: "Think of a mothership that can go out and target good brands and good companies and absorb them into an already healthy, thriving, legal and capital environment. We need virtuous private equity."

Virtuous private equity. It's certainly a good idea. And maybe a real possibility. It could be that Teamshares and A&H are just that. Brownrigg says, "We sometimes say we are putting the 'equity' back into private equity." I hope they do. They have built a strong team with admirable aspirations.

Employee ownership is like technology; it is changing all the time. But unlike technology, which always moves forward in ways that leave the past behind, employee ownership has longtime stability in many ways. It's firmly rooted—the changes are new branches on a tree rather than new plants that crowd out and make obsolete previous iterations.

Since the beginning of this book, we have been examining employee ownership and exploring stories of successions and transitions. Thanks for sticking with me. Now, in Part Three, we get to the fun part (some would say the hard part, but it really isn't that hard!) where we consider doing it! I hope you're ready for that.

PART THREE

IMPLEMENTING THE FIVE TRANSITIONS

The next three chapters are about the nuts and bolts of ownership conversion (chapter 9), next-generation leadership (chapter 10), and participatory democratic management practices (chapter 11). While these three endeavors are interdependent, they are separate processes, each of which can be addressed at a different point in the arc of a company's history.

The order of these chapters could easily have been reversed because the practices of participatory management and building leadership can get underway long before an ownership conversion takes place. But it is my view that ownership conversion is the cornerstone of the Five Transitions, and in most cases, it should be completed long before the leadership transition. And long after the events of ownership conversion and leadership transition have occurred, the cultivation and practice of participatory management will continue—for the life of the company.

These three chapters will help bring the Five Transitions to life for you and your company.

———— CHAPTER 9 ————

OWNERSHIP CONVERSION

There are many versions of small business ownership conversion. The most common are transferring ownership to family members, selling to one or more key employees, selling to a strategic buyer or private equity, becoming an employee stock ownership plan (ESOP), transitioning to an employee ownership trust (EOT), and converting to a worker co-op.

There are principles and guidelines that apply to all such conversions. Many of them are explained well in Bo Burlingham's 2014 book *Finish Big: How Great Entrepreneurs Exit Their Companies on Top*. It's a detailed examination of the steps a company should take to prepare for its next iteration, regardless of the company's type of ownership transition. If you're contemplating an ownership conversion, I recommend reading it. One of its main premises is that "as a rule, the more you care about having your business's culture, values, and modus operandi remain intact beyond your tenure, the more time you'll need to orchestrate a satisfactory transfer of ownership."[1]

If you have decided that employee ownership is your goal, the first step is to determine what kind of employee ownership. The form you will choose depends on your goals and the needs of your business and your employees. That's the first inquiry. Whether that leads to an ESOP, a worker cooperative, an EOT, or one of the newer innovations described in chapter 8, each form offers important benefits to the seller, to the business, and to the workers.

In the context of the Five Transitions and becoming a CommonWealth company, this chapter examines the process of converting to a worker co-op. If you have decided that the right approach for you to achieve these goals is to become a democratic ESOP or an EOT, you'll take a different path from the one described here. But much of the information here will apply. The only aspects that will be fundamentally different are the professional service providers you'll use and the different types of document creation and financing approaches.

Here, we will discuss:

- timing (when to do it);
- process (the steps that must be taken);
- team (service providers who manage the process);
- costs (for professional services);
- documents (that must be created);
- the new structure (once you've completed the conversion);
- the South Mountain Model (as an example of how one co-op works); and
- challenges (the hard parts).

TIMING

There are three distinct aspects of worker co-ops that must be given equal weight to ensure success: ownership, leadership, and management/governance. But these three aspects do not need to be addressed at once. The decision about when to begin ownership conversion defines the rest of the process.

Unfortunately, most ownership transitions happen when the founder or founders are ready to retire. When an ownership transition happens at that time, a leadership transition must occur as well. It is highly beneficial if ownership and leadership transitions are decoupled because each happens at a different speed, each involves a different kind of work, and each is challenging and time-consuming in its own right. One of the advantages of all forms of employee ownership is that the ownership conversion does not need to be tied to the departure of the original founder.

In most cases, the ownership conversion is easier and simpler than the leadership transition; it is more transactional. Therefore, it is advantageous if the ownership conversion is accomplished early, with a long runway to the leadership transition. This allows time to build leadership capacity and train, coach, hire, and onboard new leaders. This is true whether the new leaders rise from inside the company or are hired from outside the company. Having time to take a gradual path makes it more likely that a company will be able to develop new leadership from within.

Although I advocate for early employee ownership transitions, it's essential that the business first be mature and successful. The new employee-owners must be buying a business that is robust, profitable, and experienced, and the original owners must be selling a business that truly has value. This is a key point often missed. No matter who owns the business, leads the business, and manages the business, strong business fundamentals must be developed. This is where the *Finish Big* principles apply; a successful ownership transition depends on taking the time and focus to build a top-notch business under current ownership.

There are benefits and risks to the seller staying on after the ownership conversion. In the worker co-op world, the length of time that the owner keeps working varies tremendously. I converted South Mountain to a worker co-op at the age of 38, and our leadership transition took place thirty-five years later, when I was age 73. At Trillium Architects (chapter 4), the agreement is that the founder will stay for ten years. At PixelSpoke (chapter 3), the founder departed four years after the conversion, in his forties. When the ownership conversion and the leadership transition happen at once, the owner generally does not stay on at all or stays on only in a limited capacity.

There are clear benefits to the founder staying on for at least several years (and more if possible):

- By remaining with the company the founder might be more comfortable providing a larger share of the financing.
- The company can take advantage of the founder's leadership ability to train others and build next-generation leadership capacity.
- The new owners might reduce the risk of business missteps by keeping in place the person or persons who are likely most responsible for the company's success to date.
- Bankers will be assured by the continuing presence of the founder.
- The founder will have the opportunity to maintain and pass on the business relationships they have cultivated with vendors, trade partners, clients, the community, and other stakeholders.

- The new owners may be less sure-footed and less comfortable taking the risks that entrepreneurs would. In many cases, high-risk innovations can drive a company to new places. If the inexperienced co-op becomes hesitant to act, there may be conflict and missed opportunities.
- The company will have some assurance that the founder will not start a competing business.
- The company will enjoy some stability during a time of change.

If the founder stays on, there are risks as well:

- The founder's presence might hinder the ability of the new owners to fully grasp the steering wheel in cases where they feel ready to do so (although sometimes they might *feel* ready but not *be* ready—this is not something to rush).
- If the founder had poor relationships with stakeholders, those relationships might become more problematic if the founder continues in a primary role.
- If the founder has lost interest or wishes to be elsewhere, there's no value in their presence, and there may be significant downsides.

If your business is mature and successful and you're contemplating converting to a worker co-op, I suggest that the right time is now. Sell to the employees (and yourself) with an employment agreement that stipulates the minimum (and perhaps the maximum) number of years you'll stay, what your position and responsibilities will be, and the compensation you will be entitled to. By becoming one of the owners of the new cooperative, you are ensured of sharing in future profits. (This amount will be less, of course, than you would have received if you owned the company yourself. But who knows if the profits will increase significantly with the ownership conversion?) Some co-op conversions build in special future profit-sharing for the founder if the business becomes increasingly profitable.

THE PROCESS

Before embarking on a worker co-op conversion, I recommend that you take a sabbatical from work if you never have. You might need one anyway, and it may be the best possible way for you to assess whether you and your company are ready for conversion. Whether short or long, it's sure to clarify plenty.

Another recommendation, for both owners and employees: review the *Legal Guide to Cooperative Conversions*, published by the Sustainable Economies Law Center. It is written by attorneys but in clear, straightforward, simple language. Despite its clarity, it is still long and complex, and not everyone will have the time or headspace to digest it. There are many other good explanatory documents available on the websites of the ICA Group, Project Equity, the Cooperative Development Institute (CDI), and the Democracy at Work Institute.

Professional Guidance

In no way is an employee ownership conversion a do-it-yourself project. During this period of learning, it's a good practice to have an initial consultation with an employee ownership conversion developer for an informal assessment of feasibility and desirability and to figure out which form of employee ownership might be the best fit for your company.

The co-op developer and other professionals you hire to work with your company are important. They will manage the whole process, represent the interests of both you and the employee-buyers, and help you assemble a team of other necessary advisers and guide their participation as well.

First, you need to find a co-op developer with whom you feel compatible. Several have appeared in this book—CDI, the ICA Group, Project Equity, and the University of Wisconsin Center for Cooperatives. If you go to the Workers to Owners Collaborative website (a part of the Democracy at Work Institute), you will find them and others. Talk to a few; it's worth it. If you can't find the right fit, email me (john@abramsangell.com). We'll talk, and I'll make suggestions.

The other people you will need are an accountant, a business valuator, an attorney, and a financing partner (unless you are going to self-finance the full purchase price). In some cases, you may need a real estate appraiser or other professionals. Most consultants who do co-op conversion development regularly work with people in these professions. You will probably get the whole team of experienced professionals from whomever you hire as your primary guide. In some cases, the accountants and attorneys you already work with may know about or be interested in learning about worker co-op (or other employee ownership) structures and may be able to provide the necessary services or collaborate with the professionals your guide brings in.

In order to make a worker co-op ownership transition, the current owner(s) must first gain a basic understanding of the model and its benefits and conclude that this makes sense from their perspective. Then, a group of employees will be assembled into a steering committee to work through the process with the owner. Ultimately, a transition plan will be presented to the employees who are prospective buyers. Each individual employee must decide for themselves whether they want to purchase a share and become an owner. All of this involves significant education and changing perspectives.

Basic Steps of a Co-op Conversion

These steps originated with Rob Brown of CDI. He generously shared them, and I have paraphrased, adjusted, and added to them over time. The version presented here, in ten steps, is based on my own conversion work. In some cases, the first four steps will be conducted solely by the owner in consultation with professionals; in other cases, an existing leadership team may work with the owner. This depends on the nature of the company and the owner's wishes.

1. **Business owner or leadership team chooses a consultant to lead the process.** This should be someone with worker co-op conversion experience. If the conversion is planned to be to an ESOP or an EOT rather than a worker co-op, it should be a service provider with experience in those realms.

2. **Conduct an initial feasibility analysis.** Discuss purpose, anticipated approach, current financial and cultural condition of the company, degree of readiness, and fears and concerns. This concludes with the owner deciding whether or not to move into the full exploratory stage.

3. **Business owner decides to move forward.** Obtain an accountant's company valuation. Consider the owner's desired sale price and how to finance the purchase. Consider the owner's ongoing association with the business and what feels desirable.

4. **Create a value proposal.** This should include an introduction that describes the purpose of the undertaking; assumptions about the nature of the transaction, with as many details as possible; an analysis of a financing option, including the company's projected ability to afford the financing and to produce dividends for the new owners; and a statement of what the new co-op will be receiving (what it is buying).

5. **Organize an employee meeting to introduce the idea.** Explain worker cooperatives basics and the conversion process. Answer questions, gauge interest, and share the value proposal. If the employee reaction is positive, go to the next step. If it's negative (which is unusual, if the explanations are well presented), figure out how the communication missed its mark and try again.

6. **Organize a worker cooperative steering committee.** Create a steering committee made up of the owner, a representative group of interested employees selected by the owner, and the lead adviser. This group will conduct the work of the cooperative conversion and make the key decisions (listed in the next section). The time that each steering committee member devotes to this work should be treated as part of their job at the company and fully compensated.

7. **Reach an agreement with the current owner.** Build consensus on key elements of a purchase and sale (P&S) agreement, including price, terms, financing, management, and governance. Reach consensus among the steering committee members on whether to proceed.

8. **Make a business plan for the new cooperative.** This can be very simple if not much will change. Create or update the company mission and guiding principles.

9. **Finalize the conversion.** Create necessary legal documents, incorporate the cooperative, sign the P&S, and execute the financing and transaction agreements.

10. **Participate in ongoing worker co-op training and education.** All owners, board members, and managers of the new, cooperatively owned business work with technical-assistance providers to develop an ongoing training program to build an ownership culture and ensure future success.

It's a relatively lengthy process; selling a business always is. You may not follow this list exactly, but it's worthwhile to consult it and diverge purposefully rather than unintentionally omitting important steps.

Key Decisions

While decisions about the sale price, the financing, and the founding owner's relationship to the new co-op are essential, the following key decisions are embedded in the heart of the conversion process. These decisions, many of which will end up in the cooperative's bylaws, should be made by the steering committee. Many of these decisions are necessary for ESOPs and EOTs as well as for worker co-ops.

1. **Ownership Share Price**
   - What is an affordable but meaningful share price?
   - What is the process for purchasing a share?
2. **Eligibility**
   - How long must an employee work before they become eligible for ownership?
   - Is ownership available only to full-time employees?
   - What other qualities are required for ownership eligibility?
3. **Distribution of Profits and Member Dividends**
   - How will profit-sharing be structured and calculated, and to whom will profits be distributed?
   - How will member dividends be calculated and distributed?
4. **Board of Directors**
   - What are the responsibilities of the board of directors?
   - Who will serve as directors (specific individuals, roles, term lengths)?
   - How will directors be elected?
   - Will there be nonemployee board members?
5. **Management System Design**
   - Will management change soon? In what ways?
   - What are the current company operating policies? Do they need work?
   - Will an employment agreement be needed for the current owner(s)?

6. **Mission and Guiding Principles**
   - Does the company have a mission and guiding principles, or do they need to be developed?
   - If they already exist, do they need to be adapted?
   - Is a strategic plan necessary (three, five, or ten year)?
7. **Decision-Making**
   - What decisions will be made by the owners, by the board, and by management? Create a decision-making matrix.
   - Will decisions be by consensus? With a back-up super majority voting provision?
8. **Education and Training**
   - What kind of education and training will be needed, and who will provide it?

The Hidden Reward

As my friend Jamie Wolf became ready for retirement from his forty-year-old design/build company, Wolfworks, he and his colleagues collaborated with Rob Brown to transition to a worker co-op. In their case, they accomplished the conversion and the leadership transition at once. In this small and intimate company, that worked well.

Jamie and I have had a decades-long conversation about the nature and potential of small business, and he has a compelling observation about the experience:

As we did our homework, it occurred to me that there is a hidden reward in becoming a co-op. The responsibility to be good owners, coupled with the clear set of operating instructions the co-op must develop, leads directly to new learning. The participants begin to understand, through practice, the value of meeting effectively, the necessity of being well prepared for those meetings, the ability to listen respectfully and contribute usefully, and the tools to confront and resolve challenging issues together. Absent a commitment to ownership, that attention is generally expected of and limited to owners.

I think he said it well. This learning and capacity-building is baked into the worker co-op conversion process.

CONVERSION COSTS

I informally polled several leading co-op conversion developers about cost, and the consensus is that the whole process, in 2025, is generally in the range of $30,000 to $60,000 for professional guidance, valuation, accounting, and legal. A 2024 conversion completed by Abrams+Angell (my consulting firm, which does this work on a very limited basis) for an architecture firm cost $22,500 for our time, $13,500 for valuation and accounting, and $6,500 for legal—for a total of $42,500.

The cost range does not include payments to additional outside attorneys, accountants, or financial planners that the owner or steering committee members might choose to hire on their own for second opinions or to address personal situations related to becoming a co-op member.

In addition, you may want to have a business consultant or coach working with you to improve the overall efficacy of the business. In some cases, you may have been working with such a consultant long before you begin your ownership conversion.

Another cost to the company is the time that the owner, steering committee, and employees invest in the process. As Jamie pointed out, these costs yield significant benefits. The ownership conversion process builds a more effective company.

Once established, annual maintenance costs of the co-op are minor, but there may be ongoing fees for co-op training, education, culture building, coaching, and similar consultation.

CLOSING DOCUMENTS

The conversion process will yield several legal documents, including some, or all, of the following:

- cooperative bylaws (the governing document of the new co-op);
- asset purchase agreement (defines what the co-op is buying);
- employment agreement (may be necessary for the owner or others);
- seller capital note (the repayment agreement for seller financing);
- seller security agreement (specifying what, if anything, is securing the note);

- financing documents from lender (if owner is not financing 100 percent);
- consent resolution from seller (states that the existing owner agrees to the sale);
- consent resolution from buyer (states that new board of directors agrees to the purchase);
- articles of incorporation (new registration with the state in which the co-op is located or chooses to incorporate); and
- benefit corporation incorporation (if co-op chooses to become one).

These will be part of the closing of the sale, just like the documents produced for buying a house.

STEPPING INTO THE NEW STRUCTURE

After completing the process, what will the business be? Aside from the learning and comradery that the conversion process inspires, becoming a worker co-op makes your company philosophically and legally different from what it was before.

There are three fundamental attributes of worker co-ops:

- They are membership organizations, with membership (ownership) limited to employees who complete a trial period and invest a membership fee.
- They are governed democratically by the owners, who elect the board of directors and consent to or vote on policy matters on a one-person/one-vote basis.
- A portion of corporate earnings is allocated to owners based on their work investment rather than on capital investment. These are often called patronage dividends or member dividends, and they are in addition to normal wages and other compensation. They can be in cash or a portion may be retained by the company in "internal capital accounts." Member dividends are regulated by the Internal Revenue Service (IRS).

At their legal core, cooperatives are obligated to give members a few basic governance rights (which may vary by state), including:

- the right to an equal vote in the election of the board;
- the right to request and vote in an action to remove board members;
- the right to take part in at least one member meeting per year;
- the right of access to information about the cooperative, its members, its board meetings, and its finances; and
- the right to approve/disapprove dissolution, merger, and other major decisions.

These are important rights that keep the co-op accountable to the employee-owners. During the conversion process, as the bylaws are created, other rights, such as particular forms of mission protection, may be memorialized in the bylaws.

Board training is commonly needed, as is financial literacy instruction (if the company has not already been practicing full open-book management) and coaching in how to exercise members' new rights and responsibilities. Often, these services will be provided by the developer you have been working with or someone recommended by them. Developing these skills is essential to the long-term success of the co-op. Don't make the mistake of failing to emphasize critical member education; lack of attention to this may lead to unnecessary difficulties in future times.

For employees, ownership in a worker co-op is neither a requirement nor a right. It is a responsibility and privilege for those who want it, meet the requirements, and are accepted by existing members, which is rarely, in my experience, withheld. The idea is that if you are able to do your job well and receive positive evaluations through the waiting period, you are ready for ownership.

To illustrate how a fully formed worker co-op might look, I'll share the example of South Mountain Company (SMCo). As noted, your rendition will be different.

THE SOUTH MOUNTAIN VERSION

On January 1, 1987, I sold SMCo to a new worker cooperative corporation. I remained as president and general manager of the company (later, for reasons I can't remember, my title was changed to CEO). When it was established as a co-op, the company had ten employees and three owners (myself and two original employees). The company grew over time and stabilized at 35 to 40 employees.

Our structure has held up well. It has been adjusted over time as needed. Our transition to the next generation, in December 2022, was driven by a strong, well-aligned, younger leadership team.

The owners elect the board of directors to make policy decisions and guide the company. The functions of owners and board are delineated in the company bylaws and in a decision-making matrix. Owners, board, and leadership team have defined responsibilities.

SMCo is a democracy with clear divisions of responsibility. The board delegates much of its authority to the leadership team. SMCo makes decisions by consensus with a 75 percent supermajority backup voting mechanism in case of a stalemate. Between 1987 and 2024, only three votes were necessary.

Owner Criteria

Prospective SMCo owners are expected to meet three principal criteria:

- the intent to make employment at SMCo their primary work for the foreseeable future;
- a demonstrated ability to work and collaborate effectively; and
- a commitment to understand and honor the company's mission and guiding principles (to be good representatives of the company's purpose and culture).

Owner Responsibilities

SMCo owners have the following responsibilities:

- Pay the ownership fee.
- Serve on the board of directors at some point in their career.
- Participate in making decisions that are assigned to owners by the bylaws.
- Understand SMCo governance, financials, bylaws, and operating policies.
- Represent SMCo as a community ambassador.

Owner Benefits

The primary benfits of SMCo ownership are:

- One voice (or vote) on policy matters—owners have an opportunity to affect the decisions that chart the direction and destiny of SMCo.
- Equity sharing—all owners share annual equity distributions, partly in cash and partly in accrued value to individual capital accounts.
- Being an owner—this is an intangible that may mean more to some individuals than others; for many, it is a source of pride to be an owner rather than just an employee.

Ownership Fee

This payment, sometimes called the "membership fee" in worker co-op terminology, is for the purchase of a share of SMCo ownership. It is intended to be significant but affordable. If it were too steep, it would discourage participation, so it was originally set at the price of a good used car, which is an expense workers seem to be able to manage when necessary. At the 1987 ownership conversion, the SMCo ownership fee was set at $3,500. By 2024, it had reached $18,000, and then it was dialed back to $15,000 for at least the next five years. The ownership fee at most worker co-ops is significantly lower.

The fee may be paid at once or payments may be spread out, at no interest, for up to thirty-six months. A new owner begins to accumulate equity after at least 50 percent of the fee is paid. The fee is deposited into the equity fund; concurrently, an individual capital account is established equal to the value of the ownership fee. SMCo ownership is an uncommonly good investment. The value of the ownership fee is generally recouped through dividends in the first year or two, and equity continues to build during the term of one's employment.

Eligibility

Along with meeting the three owner criteria, eligibility for ownership requires five years of employment and a minimum of six thousand hours worked. This is an unusually long waiting period. Most worker co-ops require one to three years of employment. Periodically, the lengthy SMCo requirement has been revisited, but the conclusion has always been that it has worked well, so it has remained in place.

Equity Fund

The internal capital accounts are paper accounts that are backed by the company's net worth and, more specifically, by the company's equity fund. The equity fund provides the money to meet obligations to departing owners. The SMCo leadership team and board evaluate the fund annually to ensure that it contains sufficient capital to meet short-term and long-term obligations. Except for "Distributions while an Owner" and "Payout upon Ownership Termination" (as specified in their own sections later), equity funds cannot be used by the company for any purpose that does not produce revenue for the fund without the unanimous approval of all owners.

Individual Capital Accounts

These accountings of each owner's equity in SMCo begin with the initial ownership fee. An owner's equity increases at the end of each profitable year by means of a member dividend, would decrease if there were a loss, and continues to mature until termination of ownership. Individual capital accounts are non-interest bearing. An individual's capital account can never fall below zero, and individual owners have no liability for debt or losses accrued by the corporation.

Owner Dividends

A percentage of each year's net income is distributed as member dividends to owners, in accordance with the recommendation of company accountants and a decision of the board. This dividend is separate and distinct from the cash profit-sharing that is extended to all employees each year in the form of wage bonuses. Member dividends are based on hours worked during the previous fiscal year and paid as a combination of paper equity and cash dividends. At least 20 percent must be paid in cash (by IRS regulation), and the entire annual dividend (cash and noncash) is taxable income to each owner. Cash dividend distributions are always at least sufficient to cover the tax burden and are sometimes significantly more.

Distributions while an Owner

Individual capital accounts are not accessible until ownership is terminated, but an owner who has passed their sixty-second birthday may request payment according to the established redemption schedule. Ownership may continue for the duration of employment.

Payout upon Ownership Termination

After the close of the fiscal year in which ownership is terminated, the value of the owner's individual capital account is calculated and paid out in equal payments spread over a period of four years. A departing owner who wishes an accelerated payout or has any other special request regarding payout must receive board approval. In the case of accelerated payout, the account is devalued as follows:

- three-year payout at 90 percent of value;
- two-year payout at 80 percent of value;
- one-year payout at 70 percent of value; and
- immediate payout at 60 percent of value.

This is only one model, presented here as an example. Other co-ops have much shorter times to eligibility, lower entrance fees, different ways of treating member dividends, and many other particulars that may differ from the South Mountain model.

CONVERSION CHALLENGES

Making a worker co-op conversion is full of challenges, fears, and hurdles. Everything about the process has difficulties and rewards. It's a team effort. In many cases, it becomes a whole new aspect of your work life. The complexities are not always easy to understand and internalize. Some of it takes repetition, and years, to understand. That's why education and training are so essential, and that's why ongoing professional guidance is critical. You have questions that must be answered. In some cases, you wonder if there are questions that you should be asking that you don't know enough to ask. But with good professional guidance, the process is quite straightforward.

Sometimes the process can bring to light heretofore unexamined or unknown company weaknesses or internal resentments. The culture of readiness you've built may be less sturdy than you thought. This is not a cause for concern. It's normal, and it's an opportunity for improvement if these issues are addressed head-on in a frank and honest way.

Both founders and new owners must be able to explain the transaction to spouses and family members. It may sometimes make sense to have an attorney who represents just you to serve as a second set of eyes. But this can introduce other problems; if that attorney doesn't understand employee ownership, it may complicate matters and throw a wrench into the process. The ideal solution is to choose a transaction attorney with a great reputation who is trusted by all parties and can represent the interests of both sellers and buyers.

The democratic control in a cooperative business is, by its nature, challenging to conduct in an orderly, productive, and efficient fashion. It requires a process of cultural and business education of the employee-owners to understand roles, decision-making, risks, and responsibilities. During conversion, there must be strong bonds of trust between owner(s) and employees, and the owner(s) must be ready to relinquish control over time. Many founders, when considering their various options, are fearful of or misunderstand democratic governance and therefore may choose not to pursue the worker co-op option.

There's also the difficulty of the time that conversion work and new learning takes away from revenue-producing work. This must be managed carefully to avoid overburdening employees and negatively affecting the company bottom line. Pace yourself, and anticipate the expense in your operating budget.

There you have it. The basics of converting to one form of employee ownership. The worker co-op is not for everyone, but for those of you who thoroughly inform yourselves, get good guidance, and find your way through the thickets and tangles, facing the challenges may yield significant rewards that will transcend your tenure.

CHAPTER 10

DEVELOPING NEXT-GENERATION LEADERSHIP

W e have talked about the process of converting to employee ownership and the value of decoupling ownership conversions from leadership transitions. Ownership conversion is largely transactional, but it has educational and emotional components and growth opportunities, and it sets the stage for the leadership transition, the subject of this chapter. Leadership transitions are collaborative growth and learning processes that take time, patience, capacity-building, and frank and open conversation and deliberation. The Founder to Future journey involves significant change and can be arduous and thrilling at once. Even though the leadership transition tends to come after the ownership conversion, building leadership capacity should be part of your business development long before.

To thrive, prosper, serve, and endure, an organization needs effective leadership. Leadership—a process of social influence to maximize the efforts of others toward the achievement of goals, and to support their development—is both a skill and an art. Most everyone has *some* leadership ability, just as most everyone has *some* athletic ability, *some* musical ability, and some of every other kind of ability. Even if you say you have no musical skills at all, you can still sing a song to your child at bedtime. It's the same with leadership. Some have more leadership skill than others, just as some are better athletes and better musicians. Some people have an orientation toward leadership; they think about it and practice it. Some work hard to learn and cultivate it, while some are natural leaders. Even natural leaders often work hard to improve their skills. Many good leaders are lifelong leadership learners who observe and study examples of exemplary leadership and its principles.

The best way to lead others to dream more, learn more, and do more is to serve them. The idea of servant leadership was first brought to business practice by Robert K. Greenleaf, who became interested in the study of leadership during his thirty-eight-year career at AT&T. Greenleaf's central idea is that we can most effectively lead, and help others to learn to lead, by acting as a servant to all our stakeholders and employing principles like authenticity, integrity, honesty, compassion, empowerment, continuous improvement, strong communication, and putting others first.

Readings and trainings in servant leadership and leadership development can be valuable as you begin to think about your leadership transition. This is not about how to hire a new CEO to replace yourself; it's about how to learn to build new leadership within your company. If you want to build a hundred-year CommonWealth company, building leadership capacity must be part of your personal mission for the remainder of your career. Hundred-year companies endure because their leaders understand that they are only temporary stewards; therefore, they consistently cultivate new leadership. True leaders hire great people and build an ownership culture that is meant to outlast them.

Jim Collins is a researcher and author who has had an outsized influence on the business world. His *Built to Last* and *Good to Great* are business literature classics. He set criteria for what makes a great company and painstakingly analyzed the businesses that met the criteria to find patterns that were repeated over and over. One of the findings was that ten out of eleven great companies developed their next-generation leadership from within.[1]

But the reason to build leadership in your company is not just for succession. It's to develop a company that is truly successful and perhaps even great, right now.

THE RIGHT PEOPLE ON THE BUS

Another *Good to Great* finding contradicted the expectation that top-notch leaders begin by setting a new vision and strategy. "We found instead that they *first* got the right people on the bus, the wrong people off the bus, and the right people in the right seats—and *then* they figured out where to drive it," Collins writes.[2]

Although some of Collins's assertions have come into question over time, this core principle is durable. Get the right people on the bus. Start right now by changing your hiring practices. Hire future leaders and owners. Prioritize character over skills. We can train people, but we can't change people.

Thoroughly test your hiring choices, too. South Mountain Company has a rigorous employee evaluation process and a comprehensive path to ownership. Sometimes, as hard as it is, you must get people off the bus. This does not become easier over time (it's always heartbreaking), but the conviction about its necessity and the willingness to do it get stronger.

Sometimes, there are rewards for both parties; then it's not heartbreaking at all. Many years ago, during the early days of the internet, we had an employee who was running our woodworking shop. He was fascinated by and drawn to the internet but was afraid to take a plunge into this new domain. This tension led him to loathe his work as a cabinetmaker. One day, I invited him into my office and said, "Eric, you've got six months to figure out what you're going to do with your life."

"Wait a minute here. Are you firing me?" he said, incredulously.

"Not really," I said. "I'm gently nudging you out the door to a better future."

That nudge was all he needed. Three months later, he founded the first local internet service provider company, and he has happily worked in tech ever since. We hired a new person to run the shop who joyously came to work every morning, became a highly engaged owner, and retired after thirty years in 2022.

The right people on the bus. Start now, if you haven't already.

LEADERSHIP TRANSITION PLANNING

Once you've completed the ownership conversion (or not, in some cases) and have the right people on the bus (or at least have it partially loaded), you can start leadership transition planning. This has two aspects: preparing for the unknown and planning for the known.

No matter what stage in your business life cycle you're in, an unexpected death, disability, or other event could cause the necessity for instant leadership change. Most small businesses have no written transition plan. We all should, because these events can happen. South Mountain was in business for forty years before we wrote our first avalanche scenario: What happens tomorrow if

I'm buried in an avalanche today? This is not a long-term plan; it's for continuity, to soften the blow of a calamity and keep the company afloat. Whatever you call it—something technical, like a continuity of operations plan, or something more colorful—it's important to buckle down and do it. It should detail what happens in all parts of the company in the event of the leader's (or other key employees') demise or full disability. Be clear about who takes over their responsibilities and what capacities need to be developed.

This plan for the unexpected is an early road map for planning for the known.

What's expected and known is that every one of us who builds a company will depart someday. We have the opportunity to plan and execute a successful and graceful exit that prepares the business to thrive and carry out its mission beyond our tenure. It's a complex task distinct from ownership conversion that requires years of work.

Alex Moss, the founder of Praxis Consulting, a firm widely known for its work in employee ownership, said to me, "This is precisely why we pivoted our firm to leadership development work fifteen or so years ago. It was an acknowledgment that *structure* doesn't create leadership. Both of them take their own separate and aligned effort." A new structure alone doesn't solve inherent business problems. It requires recognition of those problems and hard work to resolve them.

FINISH BIG

In 2015, Bo Burlingham sent me a copy of *Finish Big: How Great Entrepreneurs Exit Their Companies on Top.* The book details the steps one must take to prepare a business to sell to a buyer for the highest price (and to create the most value). Although he is focused on sale, the steps he suggests are the same ones we all need to take as we prepare for our exit. Creating "value" is not just financial activity; it's also the qualitative performance of the business and its systems and people—it's work that we need always to be attending to, and well before a "sale." You should be working to create value every day, even if a sale or transition is a long way off.

After I read *Finish Big*, I wrote to Bo to tell him about our leadership transition planning and how the book had influenced my thinking:

> I thought, until I read your book, that we were well-along in this process—way ahead of schedule, in a sense. No longer do I think so. I'm

glad we still have seven years, and I hope it's enough!! I can't really say it's a wake-up call (because we have been thinking so intensely about the subject), but it definitely sharpened my sense, in many ways, of the road ahead, and helped me visualize it. I am going to be excited to share the book with South Mountain's management team. The most compelling concept for me was the idea of getting under the hood for a major tune-up—and possibly an engine overhaul—to get the business truly ready to sell. Even though we are not planning to sell, the process of working through my exit and the lofty goal of accomplishing a smooth and seamless transition seem to be identical to maximizing value and properly preparing for a sale. I'm pretty sure we need that overhaul.

Looking back at our transition planning efforts prior to my retirement, I can say with certainty that we needed that overhaul, that our Leadership Team relentlessly dove under the hood, and that the refurbishing (which is really a forward evolution) continued after my departure. The steps that lead to a good transition are the same steps that build business resilience and strength.

SOUTH MOUNTAIN LEADERSHIP TRANSITION

I briefly told the South Mountain leadership succession story in chapter 1, but there's more to tell here, and it's the best way for me to explain how to transition from first-generation to second-generation leadership.

In November 2019, at our annual whole-company Day of Business, I unveiled our board-approved transition plan. It was time to get serious with implementation. Our leadership team met regularly after that to build new capacity and gradually move my responsibilities to others.

Implementation Process

Each team member prepared a personal capability analysis and statement assessing what they could provide and what they needed to learn. We kept an evolving spreadsheet of capabilities that identified thirty-five areas of expertise, to whom each area was assigned, and the current status of the transition process for each, with scoring on a one-to-five scale (one signified not-yet-begun, five signified completed). This spreadsheet was updated and re-scored every six months. The goal was for each area of responsibility to be operating, at transition, as well as or better than it was during my tenure.

Capacity building was not limited to the leadership team—it extended throughout the company. Not only did we attempt to build great primary leadership, but we developed improved second-tier leadership throughout the company. It was a slow-rolling, thorough, evolutionary climb, and it included major changes to our management and governance systems, such as a new board structure and a decision-making matrix.

We worked together intensely during the three years of leadership transition implementation. At the end, the team was fully prepared to take the steering wheel and drive, and I was fully prepared to let it go.

At the end of December 2022, I retired, relinquished ownership, and continued to work about four hours a week (in a consulting role without responsibilities). I also agreed to serve on the board for two years. The new leadership team took the reins in full. The five people who comprise that team had each taken unlikely paths to their roles.

The Leadership Team

Deirdre Bohan, the current CEO, was hired in 1995 to replace our departing bookkeeper. She quickly mastered that job, reduced the hours required, made time to study interior design, and launched our interior design practice. Later, she was the person who stepped most effectively and thoroughly into the leadership void during my sabbaticals and led our management team after my return. She gradually matured into her leadership role and became chief operating officer and my indispensable comanager. The arc of her journey from bookkeeper to CEO has been amazing. She and I have always been highly aligned, but our leadership and communication styles are very different. In the early days, she was dependent on me. We grew together, learning from each other, and achieved a wonderful, gradual, slow-motion handoff.

Ryan Bushey is director of architecture and also responsible for sales. The founder's role as rainmaker is often one of the hardest skills to replace. Ryan is among the very best architects I've known in my career, but he had zero experience with sales until he spent several years during the transition shadowing me in sales meetings. (This shadowing was hard for me at first; I felt initially that, although necessary, it cramped my style.) Ryan soon became my very capable business development partner; by the end, we were doing sales even more successfully as a team than I'd done alone before. And we had a great time doing it.

Newell Isbell Shinn solved one of the biggest problems we ever had at South Mountain—replacing me on the production side of the business. We needed a top-notch leader for construction and the shop. Newell had all the right qualities for a production manager but almost no actual building experience. We hired him despite that, in order to get the right person on the bus. We had some rocky times, but he turned out to be the perfect fit, grew into the position, and became a truly great company leader and an important part of South Mountain's future. He is the youngest member of the leadership team.

Siobhán Mullin came to Martha's Vineyard from Ireland in 1994. She was hired in 2003 as bookkeeper to replace Deirdre and quickly became a fixture. She expanded her role to finance and human resources and became a trusted and empathetic resource for her colleagues. She was tremendously skilled and personable, but at that time she was not, in my view, a leader. She grew continuously and became our finance director. Today, Siobhán is a consummate leader, both at South Mountain and in the town where she lives.

Rob Meyers was hired as a carpenter in 1997. He liked jawin' more than sawin'. He'd be the first to tell you that he was only a so-so carpenter. It wasn't what he wanted to do, so we tried to find new roles for him where his exceptional latent entrepreneurial abilities could blossom. In 2007, we decided to seriously launch South Mountain Solar after several other tentative attempts had failed in previous years. It became the vibrant Energy and Technology department, an important profit center that pushes the company's mission forward and diversifies the business. Rob leads this endeavor with passion, competence, and connectivity, and he has become a knowledgeable and influential (and beloved) part of the solar industry in Massachusetts and nationally.

These five people have become extraordinary leaders. They came to South Mountain without the experience or the skills to do the jobs they are doing now. And they're not just doing them, they're doing them with remarkable professionalism and constant innovation, making it clear that they are well-equipped to lead the South Mountain juggernaut forward into an unpredictable future.

One of the most thrilling aspects of my job during its final years—maybe the most—was witnessing and assisting the growth and development of the people who chose to build their careers at South Mountain.

The design of my exit plan exists now as a template for future transitions. This company will never again have a twenty-five-year-old leader who remains in the role for nearly half a century because it will never again be a seat-of-the-pants start-up operation. Deirdre took the reins at the age of 55 and may stay in the role for ten or fifteen years. Hopefully, the company is developing new leadership and a robust system of transition for the next time around. Hopefully, the next CEO is already at South Mountain or will arrive soon.

Remember the idea I expressed about Deirdre becoming a "first among equals CEO"? It didn't actually go that way. It kind of did, and it kind of didn't. The five members of the leadership team became more aligned and closer than ever, but Deirdre clearly became the leader as I stepped out. She occupied that space, consulting consistently with her team, comfortably taking guidance from them, and developing into a superb servant leader. And each of the other four have capably learned to perform in the same way in their domains while they support her in her domain.

MANAGING TRANSITIONS

When you begin to plan for transition, things change. You start asking questions about the company and the people in it—questions that you never asked before or possibly never occurred to you. You become energized to make the company better and to improve business practices. You start asking questions about yourself, and everyone involved asks questions about *themselves*. Who am I? What am I doing here? What do I want?

Much of the evolutionary work that's being shepherded by the new SMCo leadership team and board emerged from that same place. We weren't just building capacity—we were uncovering deficiencies and finding opportunities.

These are all good things, and that's why it's good to get started. If you are passing on the leadership of a healthy small business, I think that a good rule of thumb is to start getting the right people on the bus at least ten years before your expected departure date (although, of course, you really want to be doing that from day one). And remember that sometimes life intervenes in unexpected ways and disrupts even the best laid plans. Maybe, for whatever reason, the day will come sooner than you think. So why not start now?

We've all heard business founders say, "I'm gonna die at my desk," or "They'll have to drag me outta here feet first." My advice: don't be one of those founders. They are often the ones who avoid thinking about succession and end up having difficult and sometimes catastrophic transitions.

Bo Burlingham says, "Building a great, enduring business is not for everyone, perhaps not for you. If it is, however, the lesson is clear. Start early."[3] He continues, "As a rule, the more you care about having your business's culture, values, and modus operandi remain intact beyond your tenure, the more time you'll need to orchestrate a satisfactory transfer of ownership."[4] To which I would add "and leadership."

As we sought help during our transition, some of the best advice we got was from a book called *Managing Transitions* by William Bridges. Bridges was an authority on change and transitions who had a fresh and wholistic way of thinking about this work. During his career, he guided thousands of people through major transitions with this advice.

Managing transitions involves helping people through three phases:

1. Letting go of the old ways and [the] old identity people had. This first phase of transition is an ending, and the time when you need to help people to deal with their losses.
2. Going through an in-between time when the old is gone but the new isn't fully operational. We call this time the "neutral zone": it's when the critical psychological realignments and repatterning takes place.
3. Coming out of the transition and making a new beginning. This is when people develop the new identity, experience the new energy, and discover the new sense of purpose that make the change begin to work.[5]

We found our way through each of these phases at South Mountain, and it helped tremendously to understand them and to be able to say, when things seemed up in the air, "Oh, yeah, this is neutral zone stuff."

Near the end of the book, Bridges says:

> If we know anything about the future, it is that it will be different from the present. *Whatever currently exists is going to change.* . . . The only certainty is that between *here* and *there* will be a lot of change. Where there's change, there's transition. . . . There's no way to avoid it. But you can manage it. And if you want to come through in one piece, you *must* manage it.[6]

Yes, you must. Practice and preparation, combined with forthright and honest communication among the leadership team and with the rest of the company, lead to confidence.

Carol Sanford, the author of *The Regenerative Business,* says about change, "There's a myth out there that people naturally hate and fear change. It's simply not true. Human beings are designed for change. It's built into the frontal lobes of our brains, which allow us to project future possibilities that we can barely resist pursuing. What people hate is the sense that change is inflicted on them— that they are victims of circumstance and have no ability to participate in shaping the future that they are being dragged into."[7]

Inclusive change requires relentless "frank, open, and honest conversation" (as the Namaste Solar folks in Colorado call it). Jon Sandler, who once served on a nonprofit board with me, says that "the health of an organization is inversely proportional to the number of undiscussables." During our transition, we purged our company of undiscussables. It was all on the table. Even if it was not always comfortable, ultimately it was always productive. The long runway we had built was essential because this was not a linear process; we had hills to climb and valleys to pull ourselves out of.

At South Mountain, it turned out that we were ready before we had planned to be. Six months before my retirement date, the six of us looked around at each other in wonder and realized that we had done this job—they were ready, I was ready, and now we had six months to polish the mirror we were gazing into. When it came time for me to retire, it was almost like I just slipped out in the night, and our six-person leadership team became five.

You've just read about a process that must happen, at some time, in every company. It's a process that happens often in large companies, which tend to have shorter leadership tenures. But in small, closely held, founder-led businesses, it is a momentous event that is often a long time in the making. It doesn't always go well. The more time and intentionality that is devoted to this transition, the more successful it will be. I think we can safely say that's a rule. And when it does go well, nothing can be more rewarding.

CHAPTER 11

PARTICIPATORY DEMOCRATIC MANAGEMENT

Ownership conversions and leadership transitions are events. They are processes that lead to a conclusion.

Participatory democratic management is different. Fundamental to CommonWealth companies, it's a practice that never stops developing, like playing an instrument or a sport. It's a set of shared learned behaviors that continually evolve. In this chapter, I describe the basics.

When a business converts from top-down to collaborative management, hierarchical structures are generally maintained but with a fundamentally different perspective. Most hierarchies serve two purposes: efficiency and maintenance of power. "Once the power aspect is gone," Terry Mollner, founder of Trusteeship Institute, once told me, "people love hierarchy because of its efficiency, and they don't find it to be a barrier to healthy relationships and a joyous workplace." It's always a step forward when hierarchy based on power is elevated to hierarchy that's based on expertise and creativity. The best ideas win. When it's really working, nobody can even remember from who had that "best idea."

My friend Robert Leaver taught me something else about power that transcends the way we mostly think about it. We think that power is like a pie—if I give you a slice, you now have more, and I now have less. But power, as Robert says, is infinite. If we share power, there is not less for us; rather, there is just more power—more for everyone.

When you create opportunities for worker participation and decision-making and invest in professional development to build leadership and management skills, employees become part of something bigger than themselves. The workplace cares for them (while they care for it) in a way that makes them proud of the place where they work and the work that they do.

Management's role changes, too. Rather than being a command center, its purposes become to reinforce company values; to resolve the inevitable conflicts that arise; to seek counsel from the employees, board, and owners; and to serve the employees. It becomes more heart than brain. As Ari Weinzweig, co-founder of Zingerman's, once said to me: "Everything we do is about believing in people and helping them to greatness."

Melissa Hoover, the Democracy at Work Institute (DAWI) founder who is now a core team member at Apis & Heritage (celebrated in chapter 8), put it to me this way: "My North Star is democratizing ownership of productive business assets and building the high engagement cultures and systems that improve people's jobs. Sometimes that means workplace democracy; sometimes it's something adjacent to that." Servant leadership and participatory democratic management can take many forms, but the heart of the matter is developing the potential of people to excel in ways that matter to them and contribute to organizational success.

Melissa listed some of the necessary components in a June 2024 keynote address at the Vermont Employee Ownership Center's annual conference. Employees need the following:

- an understanding of the business model and how to affect it;
- good rules and clear structure;
- a sense of autonomy;
- pathways to advancement;
- processes for grievances and suggestions;
- support for their lives as well as their work; and
- guidance in both how to work and what to do.

She adds that "transparency and collaboration are not inefficiencies; they drive value. It's not about business versus values. It's about values-driven business."

Carol Sanford says, "Instead of distributing tasks and information on a need-to-know basis, a regenerative business assumes that everyone in the organization needs to know the strategy and their role within it."[1]

A particularly good resource about participatory management is the "Guide to Democratic Management," produced by the School for Democratic Management. This comprehensive user guide to worker co-op operation and governance can be downloaded from the DAWI website.[2]

MISSION, PRINCIPLES, STRATEGY, AND VISION

To effectively align employees and help everyone work in harmony, a company needs a mission to describe its purpose and a set of guiding principles to emphasize its values. These should be created through the engagement of management with a representative group of employees or, even better, all employees.

When I guide a worker co-op conversion, I determine whether a mission and guiding principles exist. If they exist, we make sure they're an accurate current expression, and I help to update them if needed. If they don't exist, creating them is an important act in the conversion process.

While the mission and guiding principles describe the company's destination, a strategic plan is the map that gets you there. All three are essential components of effective long-term business practice.

A mission statement is used to explain, in simple and concise terms, the company's purpose. The statement is generally brief—either a single sentence or a short paragraph. It defines company culture, values, and fundamental goals. Mission statements communicate the company's purpose to its stakeholders—employees, clients, trade partners, media, and the community at large. Guiding principles provide a more detailed explanation of company values.

Crafting a Mission Statement

While it may be difficult to narrow down the focus of your company to a single statement, here are some tips:

- First, outline what your company does: what you produce, what service you provide to your clients, and/or something you do to make the world a better place.

- Next, describe the way in which your company does what it does. Rather than being technical, think of what values go into the core of your business.
- Finally, include why you do what you do in your mission statement. This is key. It helps you stand out as a business, highlighting what sets you apart from the others in your industry.
- Remember to keep the mission statement short and to the point.

Here are a few mission statements of some companies and organizations in this book that I find inspiring:

- *PixelSpoke:* "To help organizations create and sustain workplaces where employees thrive, leaders inspire, and businesses succeed."
- *Once Again Nut Butter:* "We hold true to our Honest-in-Trade principles and strive to provide the healthiest and tastiest products possible to our customers. We focus on integrity, sustainability, and community in everything we do."
- *ReVision Energy:* "Make life better, by building our just and equitable electric future."
- *The Industrial Commons:* "To rebuild a diverse working class in Western North Carolina, based on locally rooted wealth."

Guiding Principles

Once you have your mission statement, you can elaborate by assembling a collection of guiding principles that are more specific. Guiding principles encompass company beliefs and values and steer an organization in its decision-making. They create a company culture where everyone understands what's important. Usually, some are intended to be adhered to rigorously and some are aspirational values.

Both the mission and the guiding principles should be periodically evaluated for current relevance. And they shouldn't sit on a shelf. South Mountain Company (SMCo) first crafted a mission statement and guiding principles in 1993. Since then, both have changed several times as they are periodically reexamined during strategic planning efforts as the company develops through new phases. Every company and board meeting agenda includes the mission and guiding principles, so that people are seeing them and being reminded of them regularly. Table 1 is an example of a company mission statement and guiding principles.

Strategic Plans

Strategic plans outline an organization's long-term goals and suggest actions to achieve those goals. The most compelling part of strategic planning may not be the result but the engagement. A perfect plan is impossible. But the plan is likely to be most successful if the process to produce it is highly inclusive.

During my career, I've been involved in the creation of five-year plans, ten-year plans, fifty-year plans, and others in various public and private organizations and settings. Over time, South Mountain tried many methods that evolved to a refined and effective approach: every two years, a five-year plan is created, and every year, an update addresses tasks that need to be done to achieve the plan goals.

In the SMCo system, the annual tasks are particularly important. They are divided into overall company tasks and departmental tasks and prioritized with intended dates of completion by quarter. The leadership team examines progress once a quarter. If something has not been achieved by the expected date, it gets pushed forward a quarter (if it is not time-sensitive) or it gets prioritized (if it is). The idea is not for the plan's expectations to pressure management to get things done but to ensure that the company keeps moving its mission forward. Accountability is built into the system. And sometimes a task gets pushed from quarter to quarter until it is deemed to be no longer necessary. Maybe it was the wrong task in the first place.

The Vision

The mission, the guiding principles, and the strategic plan are all built on the vision—the foundation on which the other three rest. The vision is the statement of where you, as a company, want to be in three, five, or ten years. It's the detailed story of the future you want to create at a particular point in the future. It's fundamentally different from a strategic plan. The vision is where you want to go; the strategic plan is how you get there.

Table 1. SMCO Mission and Guiding Principles

MISSION

To uplift our community and environment by designing and building for a just future

GUIDING PRINCIPLES

People and Community	Profit and Practice	Planet and Environment
1. Create stable, meaningful jobs with competitive living wages and great benefits.	1. Align our work with our mission and guiding principles.	1. Encourage our clients to embrace our design and performance principles and goals.
2. Support our families in exemplary ways.	2. Concentrate our design and physical work on Martha's Vineyard.	2. Further our understanding and employment of regenerative principles to restore our environment.
3. Encourage workplace curiosity, creativity, health, opportunity, and fulfillment.	3. Combine beauty, craft, science, and value in our projects.	3. Implement decarbonization, climate-friendly strategies, and greater environmental responsibility and justice in our work and operations.
4. Establish enduring and respectful relationships based on mutual trust.	4. Produce work that will be loved and admired for generations.	4. Achieve net-zero energy (short term) in both projects and operations; aim for net-zero waste and toxin discharge (long term).
5. Nurture a culture of equity, inclusion, humility, laughter, lifelong learning, and collaboration.	5. Provide a superb experience for our clients from day one.	5. Contribute to the regional and worldwide transition to renewables.
6. Practice mentorship and skill development.	6. Practice transparency and open-book management.	
7. Foster diversity within our company, with our collaborators, and in our community.	7. Design for simplicity in all company endeavors.	
8. Advance our understanding and practice of worker ownership and workplace democracy.	8. Ethically source materials with a local and regional focus.	
9. Engage in civic discourse and community policymaking.	9. Honor craft and those who practice it.	
10. Actively pursue affordable housing opportunities.	10. Meet our profitability targets and share our prosperity.	
11. Share our expertise and learning with other businesses, organizations, and communities.	11. Base our business decisions on long-term thinking.	
	12. Grow only with purpose and intent.	
	13. Build future leadership.	
	14. Consider new ideas with rigor, spirit, and flexibility.	

Make sure you don't forget the vision. You'll never grow a tree if you don't start with a seed that defines what that tree is going to be.

OPEN-BOOK MANAGEMENT

Open-book management (OBM) is a key component of participatory democratic management. The term was coined by John Case in 1993 when he was writing for *Inc.* magazine. Soon after, Jack Stack, the CEO of SRC Holdings in Springfield, Missouri, wrote *The Great Game of Business*, and Case wrote *Open-Book Management*. These two books inspired a vital business movement to share financial information with all employees to encourage them to take actions to improve the company and its performance.

When employees are provided with financial information and trained to become more business literate, the new learning engages them in finding ways to help the company succeed. They begin to contribute ideas to produce improved results, their commitment increases, and they make better decisions in their day-to-day work. This is especially true when the employees are rewarded for company success through sharing profits and ownership.

When OBM was instituted at South Mountain, we gradually witnessed a growing interest in the company's financial performance. It didn't happen overnight. Implementation required consistent education to help employees develop financial literacy and constant assessment of what particular financial information is valuable. Learning how to express that information clearly, to give it context and digestibility, is essential.

It's good for morale, too, especially when workers, regardless of their place on the organizational chart, see things that leaders don't, learn how to articulate what they're seeing, and see the results of their actions. It enhances their sense of ownership and agency and makes work more fulfilling. The phrase "That's not my job" disappears from the workplace.

Countless business leaders have overcome the fear of opening the books as they witness the value of OBM. It creates additional accountability that sharpens your senses and is, in itself, a path to better performance and greater prosperity.

A corollary benefit is that open-book management, by its very nature, helps to build leadership capacity throughout the company.

MAKING DECISIONS

A critical aspect of a democratically managed company is who makes decisions and how. In a typical worker co-op, the owners make a limited number of decisions that control the corporation, like approving new owners, electing the board, and making changes to the corporate structure (e.g., changes to bylaws, dissolution or sale of company). The board of directors generally makes all decisions about company policies, growth, new business endeavors, real estate acquisition or sale, and hiring the general manager or CEO. Management prepares the owners and the board to effectively carry out their decision-making responsibilities and makes all decisions not specifically assigned to owners or board.

A decision-making matrix is a critical part of the governance of democratic companies. Like the mission and guiding principles, the SMCo decision-making chart is included in the agenda packet for every meeting of the board. Table 2 is a recent version of the South Mountain decision-making matrix.

Consensus Decision-Making

Consensus is a process of synthesizing the wisdom of all the participants into the best decision possible at the time. I'll describe how I've come to understand it and how I've used it with South Mountain and other organizations and groups. (Many advocates of inclusive consent-based decision-making adhere to a system called *sociocracy*, which was largely developed over time in the Netherlands. I've always felt that sociocracy is just another version of consensus decision-making, but it's worth a look, and if it resonates with you, by all means use it.)

Why Consensus?

There are compelling reasons for using consensus decision-making:

- Most organizations make decisions by majority rule, but that process often squelches creative thinking and leaves a minority dissatisfied.
- If the consensus decision-making process is well understood and the participants are practiced, it's remarkably efficient.
- Consensus makes a genuine effort to identify and address all significant concerns.

Table 2. SMCO Decision-Making Matrix

RESPONSIBILITIES

Owners	Board	Leadership team
Democratically control the corporation	**Oversee policies and guide the company**	**Manage company under the direction of the board**

1. Ownership and Equity
  a. Approve new owners.
  b. Determine ownership fee.
  c. Decide all equity fund-related issues, including spending from fund, patronage, and dividend distributions.
2. Board
  a. Decide the size of the board and director terms.
  b. Elect directors to, and remove directors from, the board.
3. Corporate Structure
  a. Decide all changes to the articles of organization, including:
   • Status of company as a corporation and a benefit corporation.
   • Status of company as a worker-owned corporation.
   • Name and purpose of the corporation.
  b. Decide all changes to the bylaws.
  c. Decide to merge, dissolve, or sell.
4. Borrowing
  a. Approve major borrowing.
	1. Review monthly financial reports and annual and quarterly budgets, including capital expenditures, profit-sharing, and annual allowance for wage increases.
	2. Determine company growth.
	3. Determine new endeavors and revenue sources.
	4. Decide to buy or sell real estate and to expand SMCo facilities or make significant changes.
	5. Determine philanthropy practices.
	6. Determine committee composition.
	7. Decide operating policies.
	8. Oversee strategic planning and company vision.
	9. Elect CEO and all officers of the board.
		1. Serve as the board's executive arm and report monthly to the board.
		2. Oversee staffing, including hiring, firing, internships.
		3. Evaluate individual performance issues.
		4. Determine compensation, including individual compensation specifics.
		5. Administer housing grants and stipends.
		6. Conduct capacity planning and succession planning.
		7. Oversee financial issues and budgets.
		8. Manage the project pipeline.
		9. Drive sales initiatives.
		10. Direct company communications.
		11. Coordinate professional development opportunities.
		12. Lead professional outreach efforts.
		13. Align DEI objectives with company values.
		14. Oversee path to ownership.
		15. Approve major software changes.
		16. Prepare policy proposals for board members.

- Consensus builds relationships.
- Consensus agreements tend to enjoy broader support and require less enforcement.
- Consensus moves us toward doing what is best for the common interest and prioritizes the good of the whole over any one individual.

Consensus is not necessarily unanimous agreement; participants may consent to a decision they do not agree with. It's a type of accommodation—all agree to something that they feel is best for the group or organization. The consensus includes supporters of a position, those who don't have a strong opinion either way, and those who don't fully support the position but don't have enough of a problem with it to stand in the way.

How Do We Reach Consensus?

The process of reaching consensus is guided by the meeting facilitator and involves the following steps:

- Presentation: An advocate presents a proposal, with background information.
- Discussion: The group analyzes and clarifies the information presented.
- Ideas: Group members offer, reconfigure, and synthesize ideas.
- Testing: The facilitator tests for consensus. "Is there anyone who does not approve of the group proceeding in this way? Does anyone have any serious concerns regarding this suggestion?"
- Concerns: If one or more group members have outstanding concerns, they are clarified and discussed. The group works to shape a creative solution that addresses the concerns, or the group might ask for a new proposal to be brought to the next meeting. As a solution emerges, the facilitator again tests for consensus.
- Consensus: When everyone consents to the proposal, the facilitator checks with the group to be sure the conclusion is correct, either by asking for an affirmative thumbs up, unanimous vote, or by asking if there is anyone who does not accept the proposal.

- Implementation: The group clarifies how the decision will be implemented (i.e., the who, what, when, and how).

How can someone support consensus if they have a serious concern? A central element of the consensus process is the group's careful consideration of individual concerns. Concerns are not stumbling blocks; rather, they are building blocks for crafting a decision that is wise and widely supported. If someone has a genuine concern, they raise it for consideration and then work with the group to explore creative options. If the group does not adequately address the concern, one has the power to withhold consent (known as "blocking"), thereby requiring the group to continue looking for a more acceptable course. Many organizations require that it takes two participants to block. This is the range of options for consent:

- endorsement ("I like it");
- agreement, with reservations ("I can live with it");
- stand aside ("I'm not 100 percent in agreement, but I don't feel strongly enough about this to hold up the group");
- will consent if future reconsideration is built-in ("I want to include a sunset clause or a trial period");
- formal disagreement, but willing to consent ("I want my disagreement noted in the minutes, but I will support the decision"); and
- block ("I do not consent to this proposal").

What if the group cannot reach consensus? I favor two alternatives when the process reaches a stalemate (which in well-run processes, happens only occasionally). The first is further exploration. Sometimes, faced with a difficult decision, it's good to "sleep on it" and revisit it at a subsequent meeting.

But sometimes a decision is time-sensitive, and there's no time to sleep on it. In that case, and in cases where reconsideration doesn't lead to consensus, backup supermajority voting comes into play. I think this is an essential aspect of all consensus-based organizations. Organizational bylaws should include a modified majority-rule voting procedure for use when necessary. The SMCo bylaws provide that if no decision can be reached through consensus, then a decision can be made with a supermajority affirmative vote of 75 percent—and any participant can call for a vote. In the thirty-five years of employee ownership during my tenure at South Mountain, there were three votes. All succeeded, and in each case the positive vote was significantly greater than the 75 percent required.

Zingerman's has used consensus decision-making for major decisions for thirty years. Cofounder Ari Weinzweig wrote to me:

> Consensus decision-making is not, I know, the way most people are used to experiencing democracy, and it's definitely not the way the vast majority are accustomed to working. Still, I want to posit here that after 30 years of making it work, now to the tune of $80,000,000 a year in sales, there might be a lot more to working by consensus than most Americans would be inclined to consider. Although it's not what he's well known for, Dr. Martin Luther King, Jr. understood this many years ago: "A genuine leader is not a searcher for consensus but a molder of consensus." In a belief system based around consensus, great leadership is not about big speeches, pounding the table, or boldly pronouncing orders. Rather, it's about bringing people together to talk, in the belief that, in a group that's skilled in doing this work, synergy will start to happen and that all involved will be better off for it. For 30 years now, this last line has, quietly, been at the center of the Zingerman's story.

Berrett-Koehler Decision-Making System

In business, there are endless decisions to make. Not all can be (or should be) made by full consensus, and not all fall neatly into responsibility columns. Collaborative decision-making is complicated. The publisher of this book, Berrett-Koehler (BK), has a well-developed system of decision-making guidelines that was devised by founder Steve Piersanti and has been refined and adjusted over the years.

The eighteen BK staff members use these guidelines for decisions that involve multiple staff members making decisions about an organizational policy, program, initiative, or change. The system operates by participants answering five questions to guide the process. The questions listed here, from the BK guidelines, are edited for brevity.

- *What is the decision to be made?* At the start of any discussion, the person leading a discussion clearly states the decision to be made. Others may suggest alternatives or adjustments. Disagreements about the nature of the decision are decided by the leader whose responsibility most encompasses the areas substantially affected.
- *Who is the decision steward?* This person manages the decision process. Usually (but not always) it is the person who has taken the initiative to propose something that requires one or more decisions. Disagreements about who assumes the role of decision steward are decided by the leader whose responsibility most encompasses the areas substantially affected.
- *Who should be involved in the decision?* We all make many decisions every day for which no one besides ourselves needs to be involved. The decision steward takes the lead in deciding whether to involve others in the decision and who they should be. The steward often asks individuals or groups if they want to be involved or represented. Any staff member can involve themselves in a decision by requesting that they be involved.
- *How should these persons be involved in the decision?* There are various levels of involvement:
  - Inform: People are kept informed but are not asked to give input into the decision.
  - Consult: People are consulted for input before the decision is made so that they have been heard even if the decision goes against their advice.
  - Majority vote: After discussion of a proposal, a vote is taken to approve or disapprove the proposal, with a simple majority deciding the outcome.
  - Consent: Every person involved in the decision can "live with it"—and abide by it—even though some people might decide differently if they were making the decision alone.
  - Consensus: Every person involved in the decision can say "I believe that this is the best decision we can arrive at for the organization at this time, and I will support its implementation."

The decision steward proposes levels of involvement for those involved in the decision. The default is that most decisions will be at the Inform or Consult level of involvement. To keep the process practical and time efficient, there must be compelling reasons for escalating the level of involvement to Majority Vote, Consent, or Consensus. Different people may be involved at different levels. This decision is subject to consent by the organization leader whose responsibility most encompasses the areas substantially affected.

- *What decision has been made?* The decision steward makes sure that the other four steps are followed and announces, in a timely manner to those involved, the decision that has been made.

Berrett-Koehler System in Use

BK has been using and refining this system since about 2010. Piersanti says that it is typically used several times a week, either by the whole staff or by a group or department in the company. It has become so baked into the organizational culture that they are now able to practice a shorthand version, with particular elements called out (confirming the decision to be made, who the decision steward is, and the level at which others will be involved). He adds that this process is sometimes taken for granted; some people don't realize how different it is from standard hierarchical organizational decision-making. The biggest problem is when people forget about it, dive right into decision-making without following the steps, and then run into issues that could have been avoided if the model had been followed. Some feel the system is too cumbersome and avoid it, but that is a minority point of view.

The current CEO of Berrett-Koehler, Praveen Madan, is a great champion of the system. He learned it when he was a BK board member and used it at another company he ran, Kepler's Books, before he took the management reins at BK.

The perception that consensus decision-making is inefficient generally comes from those who have not yet learned the skills or experienced the benefits. Shared governance is certainly challenging, as are all democratic processes, but good leadership and training can turn the challenge to promise and efficacy. Those aspects of consensus decision-making that sometimes make the process slower often serve to improve the quality of the decisions by making more information available to more stakeholders and building trust. Over time, the process speeds up as participants gain skills.

Another component of a good decision-making process is learning to conduct good meetings.

UTTERLY PRODUCTIVE MEETINGS

Meetings are the pots in which ingredients are mixed to make satisfying organizational stew. They are one of the most important ways we get work done. Good meetings empower, enliven, and inspire us. Poor, unfocused, dysfunctional meetings feel boring, waste our time, and confuse us—they make sloppy stew.

Good meetings are the heart of our communication with each other, and they reinforce our culture—in fact, they are one of the ways to develop and refine organizational culture. Good meetings do not happen by chance. We can ensure utterly productive meetings by building the capacity to facilitate, to participate effectively, and to engage in satisfying and inclusive collaborative decision-making.

I have always been amazed that good meeting practice and meeting facilitation skills are not taught in school. We all spend large parts of our lives in meetings, so it makes sense both to learn how to guide (facilitate) meetings and how to be a good participant. The elements of a good meeting are the same, whether the meeting is in person or conducted remotely.

Meetings are generally efficient, productive, inclusive, and satisfying when these conditions are met:

- there are agreements about the "rules of the road" beforehand;
- the agenda and goals of the meeting are clear to everyone;
- one task is dealt with at a time;
- everyone remains focused on the task at hand;
- each person's input is heard and acknowledged;
- everyone has equal power in making decisions;
- decisions are made to which all consent;
- everyone is clear about necessary follow-up at the end of a meeting; and
- at meeting's conclusion, there is a time for participants to offer appreciations.

Meeting Facilitator

The facilitator leads the meeting by helping the group to clarify and move through its agenda in a clear, respectful, and timely manner. The facilitator serves as the driver, a "meeting chauffeur." Typically, a facilitator performs these tasks:

- develops the agenda for the meeting in consultation with all participants or representatives;
- ensures that the meeting space is in order (e.g., chairs, lighting, tech, sound, flip charts) or, if a remote meeting, that all have the proper link and access;
- convenes and adjourns the meeting in a timely manner;
- helps the group move through its agenda, focusing on one item at a time;
- makes suggestions to encourage an open and balanced flow of discussion;
- helps the group gain deeper understanding, by asking questions such as, "What made you say that?" or "Say more about what you mean" or "Thanks for that suggestion—what benefit do you think would come from doing that?";
- intervenes when there are interruptions, distractions, or overly long comments;
- asks clarifying questions and makes suggestions, but does not make decisions;
- occasionally summarizes points of agreement and points of divergence and asks for reactions to the summary so that the group can move ahead ("Did I get that right?");
- occasionally uses straw votes to take the temperature of the room;
- assists the group through its established decision-making process;
- tells the group when it has arrived at a decision and asks for agreement ("Does that sound right?");
- helps the group plan follow-up, clarifying who, what, when, and where;
- makes sure that the minute-taker has a record of all action items; and
- if necessary, relinquishes responsibilities to another (a co-facilitator) when the facilitator needs to contribute to the meeting *content* in a way that makes it difficult to be fully attentive to the meeting *process*.

Good facilitation often goes unnoticed because it leads to seamless meetings: we gathered, we greeted each other, we proceeded through an agenda with good spirit and feeling, we made clear decisions, we made commitments, we expressed appreciations, we said good-bye, and we left the meeting. It's a simple as that, but it requires practice and skill.

Meeting Participants

Every participant is either a beneficial or detrimental force. No one can simply "attend" a meeting. Participants improve the quality of the meeting when they agree to do the following:

- review all meeting materials before arriving at the meeting;
- arrive on time;
- engage fully in discussion, mindfully keeping comments brief so that all have an opportunity;
- remain solution-oriented without being attached to any one particular outcome;
- listen carefully and respectfully when others are speaking, no matter their viewpoint;
- accept that "information" comes in many useful forms—facts, opinions, hunches, ideas, feelings, mistakes, and silence;
- voice concerns in a respectful manner that invites constructive response; and
- understand and take part in the decision-making process used by the group.

The Agenda

A meeting agenda is an outline of the topics to be discussed by the group and the order of discussion, often with times assigned to each item:

- Before the meeting, the facilitator develops this plan in consultation with meeting participants or representatives. This advance preparation reduces the likelihood that a meeting gets bogged down by too many unforeseen issues or vague topics.

- Agendas are distributed to all meeting participants in advance.
- When the meeting begins, the agenda is reviewed and adjusted by the participants. Then the group can proceed with this road map, making further adjustments as necessary.

The Minutes

Minutes are the written record of the meeting. They begin with the name of the meeting, when and where the meeting was held, who attended the meeting, who was absent, who facilitated, and who was the minute-taker.

- Minutes are not a transcript but rather a concise summary of key points raised, decisions made, next steps, doers, and deadlines.
- Minutes should use polite and clear language and avoid acronyms.
- Minutes are typically reviewed at the following meeting of the group, at which time corrections can be noted for the record and the minutes receive formal approval.
- Draft meeting minutes should be distributed within twenty-four hours of the conclusion of the meeting so that those who are responsible for follow-up have the guidance they need.
- Like facilitation and participation, good minute-taking is a skill that must be learned and practiced.

Meeting Reminders

This checklist can help make meetings more efficient, productive, and satisfying.

Before the Meeting

- Do your homework. Read your materials in advance.
- Don't come with "the plan." Come with an idea or proposal and see where the group takes it.
- Arrive and get settled early enough so that the meeting can start on time.

During the Meeting

- Help the group stay focused on the agenda.
- Help the group create space for everyone to participate.

- Listen attentively ("active listening"), and work hard to understand what others are saying.
- Be patient and respectful.
- Accept that information comes in many useful forms—facts, opinions, hunches, ideas, feelings, mistakes, and silence.

When Speaking

- Be concise.
- Express one idea at a time.
- Use "I" statements to define your needs.
- Own your feelings.
- Give the reasons behind your thinking.
- Take a dose of humility.

When Deliberating

- Take a long-term view.
- Be open to outcome.
- Don't lobby your idea.
- Don't set limits.
- Look fairly and equally at all pros and cons and encourage others to do the same.
- Learn when to let go.

At the End and After the Meeting

- Evaluate: "What worked?" "What could we have done better?"
- Assign commitments: "Who's doing what, by when?"
- Share appreciations.
- Follow-up on commitments assigned to you.

Good meetings are good stuff. No doubt about it. They improve the quality of our lives and work. In a democratic organization, it's important to train participants in consensus decision-making and good meeting processes.

SOUTH MOUNTAIN'S "PATH TO OWNERSHIP"

It's also important to fully prepare employees for ownership. For much of our history at SMCo, we did this in an ad hoc way. The techniques and systems in this chapter are part of developing an ownership culture and learning to practice participatory democratic management efficiently and effectively. But there is more to preparing individuals for ownership.

In 2022, after two years of design, the formal SMCo path to ownership was unveiled and put into practice. CEO Deirdre Bohan says, "Becoming an owner has historically happened mostly by osmosis; by the time you had been at SMCo for five years, you were assumed to know what you needed to. We wanted to encourage more active preparation, hoping that would develop more engaged owners." The path to ownership has now been incorporated into the employee onboarding process so that new hires start it on their first day of work.

The path includes thirty-three supervised experiences designed to give new employees, over a seven-year time span (five before ownership, two after), a complete picture of what South Mountain is, how it works, and how to be an effective owner. The purpose is twofold: to develop active and engaged SMCo owners and to strengthen relationships within the company.

Communications coordinator Abbie Zell led the development process with a team that included Deirdre, Siobhán Mullin, and me. Abbie says, "We chose Path as the central metaphor because it has a clear beginning, can meander, has progress markers along the way, a guide when necessary, and a reward at the end."

The Trail Map is a physical manifestation of the path. It is the size and style of a national park passport and works along the same lines. Each new employee gets one; when they complete an experience, it is initialed by their instructor. When there are no experiences left, they will be a seasoned South Mountain owner! You can see the SMCo Trail Map and read more about the Path to Ownership on the company website.

Experienced employee-owners guide participants through their areas of expertise, and Abbie oversees the program and acts as liaison between participants and guides. Some of the activities are done as a cohort, some are done alone with guidance.

At the inaugural meeting of the program, with all 18 non-owner employees in the room, Abbie distributed the $4'' \times 5''$ trail maps and explained their significance. There was palpable excitement in the room. Abbie's joyous presentation style provokes that, but the concept and content speak for themselves. One employee said, "It was so great to gather and be exposed to that so early in my tenure. I love the passports—classy and tangible—that we will use to chart our course." Another, who had just been hired, said that it made him feel that he had joined an organization that doesn't perceive him as a worker, but rather as a member of a community.

This new initiative makes the experience of being an employee (and an employee-owner) richer and more complete. It builds trust, encourages cross-pollination, and spreads knowledge across the company's four departments. It prepares developing leaders and new owners for the future in an intentional way.

It's a lot of fun too.

AND THEN THERE'S THE MONEY

Another thing that must be managed, cooperatively, is the wealth that is created. At South Mountain, net profits are used for four discretionary purposes: capital expenditures and improvements, capital reserves, the equity fund that pays departing owners, and employee compensation. The drive to direct as much as possible to employee compensation leads to carefully considered reckoning with the first three purposes.

There are four ways employees are compensated:

- Wages and salaries
- Benefits (as described in the SMCo operating policies)
- Profit-sharing (provided to all employees, in cash, based on hours worked)
- Member dividends (provided to owners only, part in cash and part as equity obligation, again based on hours worked)

Because profit-sharing and dividends are based on hours worked rather than pay rate, they partially mitigate the hierarchical wage scale (which already has a very low top-to-bottom ratio). The leadership team decides the amount of profit-sharing, and the owners decide the amount of dividends (usually ratifying recommendations by the company accountants) and the portion that will be paid in cash.

The Internal Revenue Service (IRS) requires that at least 20 percent of the dividend be paid in cash. SMCo has always made sure to distribute enough in cash to at least cover the corresponding tax obligation. (Each owner must pay taxes on the dividend in the year that it is awarded—later, when the equity is paid out, it is not taxed again.) The cash part of SMCo dividends has varied from 35 percent to 50 percent.

Compensation Philosophy

This is the SMCo compensation philosophy (reprinted from the SMCo operating policies, which are publicly available on the company website, as are many other SMCo documents):

At SMCo, we hire for long-term employment and worker ownership.

Our compensation packages are designed to meet the needs of employees at many stages of their lives and rely on a total-rewards model, of which competitive wages are a key part. We also focus on work/life balance, generous time off, 401K match, housing and electric vehicle grants, professional development opportunities, industry-leading health benefits, and more.

Additionally, our profit-sharing program distributes a portion of the company profits to all employees, and our worker-ownership model distributes member dividends designed to build long-term wealth among SMCo Owners. Both programs are based on the hours each employee works, not on their wage rate, position of the org chart, or longevity.

We strive to maintain a total compensation ratio from highest paid to lowest paid that is no more than 4 to 1, and we commit to paying staff fairly and justly relative to each other.

We increase all wages annually through cost-of-living adjustments (COLA). Performance is rewarded by progress raises based on skill development and mastery, level of responsibility, recent past performance, and training. One-time bonuses celebrate each year's achievements. We have transparent wage scales that are accessible to all staff.

We generally promote from within, incentivizing career and compensation pathways to move up.[3]

Dividends and Equity Fund

Generally, SMCo dividend distributions are roughly 50 percent of the remaining net income after profit-sharing. They are limited by IRS regulations. The goal is to maximize dividends so that earnings go to employee-owners rather than to the IRS (these distributions are a deductible expense). They are tracked in internal capital accounts and reflect the equity that each owner has earned—their individual share of the value of South Mountain Company.

Internal capital accounts are company obligations to employee-owners that accumulate over time and are paid out upon termination of employment (people still working at age 62 can choose to begin taking their payments while they are still employed).

In the mid-1990s, we decided it would be prudent to start putting money away in order to build a single-purpose equity investment fund to back up our obligation. Mike Drezner, one of our early owners—a carpenter and a knowledgeable stock market maven—managed the fund with me and my old friend Christina Platt, a socially responsible investment adviser at Morgan Stanley. Gradually, responsibility shifted from me to Mike, and for many years Mike and Christina managed the fund together. In 2000 (when our obligation was $877,000 and the investment fund contained $72,000), we resolved to increase our contributions and build the fund until it contained—at all times—assets equal to at least 50 percent of our obligation. It had become clear to us that one of our primary responsibilities as owners was to honor our equity obligations for decades to come. By the end of 2004, we reached our goal: there was $1,050,000 in equity obligations and $550,000 in the fund.

When Mike began to approach retirement age, he trained Siobhán Mullin, our bookkeeper (now financial director), to take over. In 2012, Siobhán and Mike developed a twenty-five-year spreadsheet that made a series of assumptions and projections about retirement dates, fund contributions, and fund earnings to help us determine how aggressively we needed to build the fund over time. It's essential that we have the right amount of money to satisfy long-term obligations (similar to Social Security). Because this pot of money has a sole purpose (paying off former owners), it's important not to overfund it. Doing so would tie up cash needlessly and make it unavailable for other important uses. But if there's too little cash, we may not be able to meet our obligations in future years. This is the central tension of the equity fund.

The spreadsheet is examined each year, assumptions are adjusted as necessary, and funding decisions are made by the board and included in each annual SMCo budget. Generally, contributions from company cash flow are in excess of $100,000 per year.

The equity fund has been skilfully managed by Mike, and then by Siobhán, with our Morgan Stanley advisers. Siobhán now works with a third-generation adviser from the same office. These financial advisers have served the company, and individuals within it, in ways that go beyond managing the equity fund and the pension fund. Every year or two, our Morgan Stanley adviser, Deb Tharp, sets aside time to do an individual personal finance planning session with any SMCo employee who signs up for one.

One of the most compelling aspects of the fund is the balance between safe investing and impact investing—seeking investments that are truly consistent with our mission and values and looking for low-risk mission-aligned investment opportunities.

Without the approval of 100 percent of the owners, equity funds cannot be used for anything except their stated purpose—paying out obligations to departing owners. Any use other than that must be for something that will return income to the fund. In 2009, to create work in recessionary times, we invested $125,000 from the fund in a property on which we built a zero-energy house on speculation. The project generated much-needed work, and when the house was sold, the fund was paid back with a healthy chunk of interest from the proceeds.

Many employee-owners have reached the end of their careers and retired in recent years. In June 2024, the fund was paying out nine prior owners who had departed over the years. At the time, the fund had obligations to current and past employees of $2.6 million and assets of $1.5 million (57 percent).

SMCo also manages a 401K pension fund for employees. Individuals contribute and the company matches with 3 percent of wages. This fund had assets of approximately $8 million in June 2024. Like the equity fund, it is managed by

Siobhán and Deb, but it's easier to manage because the amount of money in the pension fund always equals the obligation.

Meanwhile, each of the SMCo owners continues to earn equity every day they work. Wages, benefits, profit-sharing, and equity—all contribute to SMCo owners' earnings.

SMCo is an example of how one successful company manages its money. Everyone does it in their own way. Your inclinations may be entirely different, but the fundamental principle is that all democratic companies should have well-documented and well-communicated approaches to compensation and distribution of profits.

COMPETITION AND COLLABORATION

More than a half century after starting South Mountain Company, I still believe, with more conviction than ever, that collaboration always trumps competition. This appears to me to be true in both nature and society, even though the opposite message—that competition is desirable and unavoidable—is drummed into us from preschool to graduate school to the workplace.

About twenty-five years ago, I read *No Contest: The Case against Competition*, by educator and social theorist Alfie Kohn.[4] Kohn has been described as the country's leading critic of competition (although he is said to be quick to point out that there is little competition for the title). In his thoughtful and well-researched critique of our winner-loser society, he shatters myths regularly. He argues that competition systematically damages relationships and crushes self-esteem. Most competitors lose most of the time because, by definition, not everyone can win. The race to win turns most of us into losers, and as comic Lily Tomlin once quipped, "The trouble with the rat race is that even if you win, you're still a rat."

When confronted with the question of eliminating competition in favor of cooperation, people tend to say that we can't possibly keep our world exciting and productive without competition, which is everywhere in our society—in business, politics, sports, and academics. Competition has helped us to scale great heights, we're told.

My experience has taught me, however, that we do better across a multiplicity of goals, producing greater, more lasting satisfaction, and greater happiness, when we work in cooperative modes, balancing the needs of multiple stakeholders. People in an equitable and cooperative setting will attain goals with more creativity than people in a competitive setting, and they'll have a better time doing it. Building the culture of the democratic workplace, in my view, maximizes vitality with a minimum of rivalry and contention.

Effective participatory democratic management is not easy to construct and practice, and it requires constant refining. There are as many versions as there are organizations. But, in my experience, the payback is immense. Are you, in some way, working on this important Five Transitions element in your business?

CONCLUSION

Building the CommonWealth Economy

This book is about implementing the Five Transitions to become a CommonWealth company. Its *purpose* is something else: to make CommonWealth companies commonplace, and to demonstrate that business can lead the way to the restoration of democracy. My hope is to influence some of the three million business founders who are fifty-five or older, and those who are younger as well, to take an uncommon business succession path and to make uncommon commerce common, we might say.

Along with educating and influencing business founders, another core purpose is to educate the millions of people who work in those companies, who have helped to build them, and whose lives depend on the stability and endurance of the businesses. Employees are reaching for fulfillment, honesty, and meaning in their work. They want to make good livings and share the wealth they help to produce. If they knew more about employee ownership options, they might be able to introduce these options to their employers.

The Berrett-Koehler constitution says: "We are embarked together on a journey to do the seemingly impossible—to create a world that works for all. No road map exists for this journey, so we are drawing one as we go, marker-by-marker."

That may express the purpose of this book even better. It is a road map to a world that works for all. Carol Sanford says, "The best way to keep people happy and healthy is to provide them with opportunities to express their potential in service to something greater than themselves ... I believe deeply that the renewal of democratic institutions depends on growing the innovative capacities of businesses."[1]

Could employee ownership achieve significant wealth-sharing the way unions did in the middle decades of the 20th century? Could we achieve the aspirational goal of 40 million American employee-owners by 2040? My hope for this book is to (modestly) intervene in our economic system—toward changing its goal to serving stakeholders (particularly workers) before shareholders (investors). And to make work more purposeful, meaningful, and rewarding. As my friend Tom Chase says, "If you're trying to fix a broken clock, the goal isn't to set the hands to the current time; it's to make it work it again." Let's do that with our economy, to whatever degree it's possible.

FROM HOPE TO OPTIMISM

Employee ownership trust advocate and educator Mark Hand described to me a meeting he had with a significant number of small business owners to discuss ownership succession. "What I found in practice," he said, "listening to founders and owners, was that they were not comfortable using the language of [workplace] democracy. And I think that's because people associate it with anarchy and socialism."

A democratic workplace and shared ownership have nothing to do with either anarchy or socialism, at least as people commonly, and mistakenly, use those two terms in the United States today. We need to dispel that myth, because workplace democracy is actually a stronger and broader expression of capitalism because it expands the system to value more than profit. The CommonWealth company is about making an inclusive economy that works for all (which ours currently does not), just like our democratic political system should ensure liberty and justice for all (which ours currently does not). Both ambitions, in my view, should be among our highest priorities as individuals, as a society, and in business.

Does it seem far-fetched to imagine that we can make this new economy? I am *cautiously optimistic* that over time we can, but I am *absolutely hopeful*. Optimism and hope are different. Former Czech president Václav Havel once said, "Hope is definitely not the same thing as optimism. It is not the conviction that something will turn out well, but the certainty that something makes sense, regardless of how it turns out."[2]

Business owners worry that their employees won't be able to run their business. I hope I've left you with the sense that, with proper training, it's usually the case that they can. Founders worry that they won't get a fair price if they sell to employees. I hope I've shown that they do. They worry that the process is complicated and difficult. I hope I've shown that employee ownership conversions, with competent guidance, can be no more complex than any other kind of ownership transition.

We need to reach those business owners who are not comfortable using the language of democracy. We need to figure out where and how to engage them, and we need to bring unfamiliar but potentially appealing (if effectively communicated) ideas and information to them. We need to show them that employee ownership and workplace democracy are practical avenues to good business and long-term mission protection. We can roll up our sleeves, get out there, and turn hope into optimism.

THE PEOPLE IN THIS BOOK

The stories in this book, offered to me by generous people who were excited to tell them, are stories of success, innovation, and good businesses that work for all and change lives. There are many more stories beyond those you've read. Here's one I haven't yet told that I find particularly inspiring.

Brett Tolley is a fisherman in Chatham, Massachusetts, on Cape Cod. As he tells it, "Five or six of us were sitting around a living room in 2017, lamenting the state of the local fishery, the buyers who kept sinking prices, and our limited ability to earn a decent livelihood doing the work we love." They considered setting prices among themselves. A local attorney told them that would be price-fixing, but they could engage in legal collusion if they organized a cooperative and everyone sold through the co-op.

They did. As of this writing, twenty fishermen own and operate the Chatham Harvest Cooperative and share in the decision-making and profits. The attorney's knowledge of cooperatives changed the trajectory.

"Everything centers around the fishermen," Tolley said. "Our idea is to move fishermen from being 'price takers' to 'price makers,' to build a supply chain that has a fair price paid to the fishermen and a fair price offered to the local community."

The Chatham Harvest Cooperative offers fresh, local fish year-round through memberships in its community-supported fishery. It has begun to educate consumers about abundant underused species. "When people buy from us, they know who caught it, where the money is going, and that we are actively doing right by the ocean and its ecosystem. Our mission is to use fishing as a force for good."

These stories of success may be the most powerful educational tool we have. We can bring them to business owners and workers across America and beyond who are unaware of the employee ownership succession strategy and might therefore close their doors or sell to strategic buyers or private equity.

To get to 40 million employee-owners by 2040, we need to keep telling these stories. My hope that we can succeed is bolstered by the extraordinary array of people doing the great work of spreading the word, guiding transitions, researching, training, passing legislation, providing financing, refining models, and experimenting with new forms of employee ownership.

Colorado employee ownership attorney Jason Wiener said to me, "I get the most excited about the least sexy, least interesting interventions that twist a dial that an existing business or an existing community is already working with. It may mean, for example, that a community thrives around a certain SBDC [small business development center]. So, we get this one SBDC coach to understand employee ownership, and they share the gospel with a hundred people in a rural town. Now we are talking about influencing the changing fate of an aging—and potentially dying—rural community. That's what I love."

Me, too.

SBDCs. Chambers of commerce. Rotary clubs. Business association conferences. Small business gatherings of all kinds. Every business school in the country. These are the right places for this message. Maybe the Five Transitions and the idea of the CommonWealth company can be persuasive. But maybe these ideas are too radical for some people. That's fine, too. The spectrum of employee ownership options allows for an infinite number of manifestations and solutions. One of them will probably work for you.

I've been clear about my preference for the worker co-op. That's probably because I lived it, for thirty-five years, every day, and it's the form of ownership and governance I can speak about with the most certainty and familiarity. It's like living in a place and reaching an age where you realize you can never know another place to the extent and depth that you know the one you've lived in for so long. I know the worker co-op that way.

That being said, my affinity for the worker co-op in no way dampens my enthusiasm for other forms of employee ownership done well. If companies offer broad-based, long-term employee ownership, if they share the wealth that is the product of the employees' work, and if they provide workers with a governance voice, then they are doing the job, no matter what the form.

When workers are sailing on the ship that they've built and charting its course, great things can happen to the economy, our democracy, and the quality of people's lives. The benefits of the democratic workplace may aid and influence the essential repair of our battered and fractured civic landscape—it could change, in effect, the symmetry of our culture. If you spend your days working in an environment of collaboration, mutual respect, and shared power and are compensated well, it is bound to spill over into other parts of your life—better parenting, more civic engagement, kinder relationships, greater tolerance.

Could we—through education, publicity, and storytelling—cause employee ownership to become the number-one business succession planning option?

FROM FOUNDER TO FUTURE

That's the plan. Now it's time to act.

I hope that you now know that it's possible to change your business and your workplace in ways you may not have imagined previously. If this book is reaching the people I hope it is, you are undoubtedly a special person. You have spent decades building a small business you love. You are getting ready to retire, or you want to work another ten to fifteen years and realize that now is the time to start planning for early ownership succession.

Or you are an employee of one of those businesses and care deeply about your job and the company you work for. You want it to endure, and you want more of a stake. Back in 1986, two of my long-time employees came to me and stimulated me to pursue the worker co-op option—that changed the arc of the company's history forever. Perhaps you could introduce this book, and the ideas contained herein, to the owner of the business where you are employed.

Your business is an anchor in the community where you live, whether it's in Georgia, Oklahoma, Michigan, Oregon, New Hampshire, Virginia, or any one of the other forty-four states, or maybe Canada or Mexico, Italy, Korea, India, or another country. You hope this remarkable business you have made—this dry cleaner, software company, specialty manufacturer, grocery store, tire shop, brew pub, lumberyard, drugstore, insurance agency, plumbing company, coffee roaster, organic farm, appliance store, or whatever else it may be—will endure and continue to serve its customers, its community, and the employees who have helped you to build it. Your kids may not want to take charge of the business; they are likely to have other things on their minds.

You are the right person to take a fundamentally different path from the one that most small businesspeople take. You are the right person to begin to engage in the Five Transitions to steer you toward CommonWealth.

You are the right person to enact a succession plan. You are the right person to invite your employees to a fruitful shared future. You are the right person to convert your business to employee ownership.

You are the right person to become the next Founder to Future story.

FROM FOUNDER TO FUTURE DISCUSSION GUIDE

INTRODUCTION

- After reading the Introduction, what did you hope to learn from this book?
- When small businesses function at their best, what does that look like for employees, for owners, for customers, for the community, and for the world?
- What prevents small businesses from functioning at their best?

PART ONE

- The author shares stories and resources that influenced his perspective on how business could serve as a tool for improving the lives of employees and the wider community. What experiences and resources have shaped your perspective on the role of business in the world?
- How do the guiding principles of your company affect the company's employees? How do they affect the company's customers? How do they affect the wider community?
- What guiding principles (existing or new) would you like your company to protect and carry forward for the benefit of future employees, customers, and community?
- How is your company's approach similar to that of South Mountain Company, and how is it different?

- The author suggests that building a small business is like building a cathedral—both are projects of care to benefit the larger community and future generations. How do you feel about making business decisions based on values other than short-term profit?

- Do you currently have a business succession plan?

- What is the mission of the company that you own or work for? Is this a mission that energizes you in your work each day? If not, how might that mission be improved?

- Have you done the B Corp assessment? If so, what did you learn from it?

- The author shares the stories of three different mission-driven companies (Dean's Beans, Snow River, and Zingerman's). Which story interests you the most and why?

- The author suggests that the "gospel of growth" deserves to be challenged. What aspects of your company should grow more and why? What aspects should be limited and why?

- Why does the author think business longevity is important? Do you agree?

PART TWO

- The author shares many benefits of worker co-ops (benefits for owners, for employees, for the business, for the community and the economy, and for durability). Which benefits are of particular interest to you and why? Are the benefits convincing?

- If you have some familiarity with a particular worker co-op, what benefits have you observed or heard about? What matters of concern or unclarity would you like to learn more about in that worker co-op structure?

- In chapter 3, the author shares the stories of two companies that became worker co-ops (PixelSpoke and Ward Lumber). What is one point of particular interest in these stories and why? What is one point of potential concern and why?

- The author notes that "conversion to a worker co-op is not uncomplicated," but good consultants and a financing plan can smooth the way. What is a particular concern you have about establishing a worker co-op? What feels like a risk to you?

- The author explores misconceptions about the worker co-op brand and leadership structure. What stories or opinions have you heard that concern you about worker co-ops? Does the author's treatment of the misconceptions allay your concerns?
- In your field, industry, or community, are you aware of any companies already structured as a worker co-op? If so, how might they be helpful in your exploration?
- The author shares stories of several worker co-op networks (Mondragon, Emilia-Romagna, The Industrial Commons, the Namaste Network, Building Energy Bottom Lines). Which story interests you the most and why?
- Are you aware of any networks of businesses in your community or region that might support companies undertaking the Five Transitions? If so, how might they be supportive?
- As you consider the wider field of alternatives for how employee ownership might be structured, which option interests you the most and why? Which option is of the least interest to you and why?
- What aspects of ESOPs do you find most and least attractive?
- What aspects of employee ownership trusts do you find most and least attractive?
- Which of the innovations in chapter 8—direct share ownership, worker cooperative holding companies, Teamshares, Apis & Heritage—do you find most compelling? Why?
- Which of the above do you think has the most long-term US potential? Why?
- Do you think private equity's new interest in employee ownership is beneficial or detrimental? Why?

PART THREE

- The author outlines a variety of key decisions that are part of the conversion process. If you were to embark on this process, which decision would concern you the most and why?
- How do you weigh the challenges versus the benefits of converting to employee ownership?

■ The author suggests that ownership conversion and leadership transition are two distinct processes and that ownership conversion can happen much sooner. How do you feel about separating these two matters?

■ The author offers suggestions to support participatory democratic management, especially in regard to conducting meetings and making decisions. Which suggestions are especially useful to you and why?

CONCLUSION

■ If you find the possibilities in this book helpful, how might they best be shared with others?

■ If you are an owner or an employee, what "next steps" does this book inspire you to consider?

NOTES

INTRODUCTION

1. "Small Business Closure Crisis," Project Equity, accessed May 17, 2024, https://project-equity.org/impact/small-business-closure-crisis/; "Business Owners' Ages," United States Census Bureau, last modified September 25, 2020, https://www.census.gov/library/visualizations/2020/comm/business-owners-ages.html; "What's New with Small Business," Small Business Administration Office of Advocacy, last modified March 2023, https://advocacy.sba.gov/2023/03/14/whats-new-with-small-business/.

2. Kevin Lindsey, Nathan Mauck, and Ben Olsen, "The Coming Wave of Small Business Succession and the Role of Stakeholder Synergy Theory," November 8, 2017, http://dx.doi.org/10.2139/ssrn.2925608.

3. David Korten, *The Great Turning* (San Francisco: Berrett-Koehler, 2006), 201.

4. The three million figure is from "Small Business Closure Crisis."

5. "Labor Force Statistics," US Bureau of Labor Statistics, accessed August 8, 2024, https://data.bls.gov/cgi-bin/surveymost?ln.

6. Lawrence Mishel and Natalie Sabadish, "CEO Pay and the Top 1%: How Executive Compensation and Financial-Sector Pay Have Fueled Income Inequality," Issue Brief 331, Economic Policy Institute, May 2, 2012, https://www.epi.org/publication/ib331-ceo-pay-top-1-percent/.

7. Robert Leaver, *The Commonwealth Organization* (Providence, RI: New Commons, 1995).

8. Corey Rosen and John Case, *Ownership* (Oakland, CA: Berrett-Koehler, 2022), 81.

9. "Make Business a Force for Good," B Lab, accessed April 15, 2024, https://www.bcorporation.net/en-us/.

10. Ibid.

11. John Abrams, *The Company We Keep* (White River Junction, VT: Chelsea Green, 2005); John Abrams, *Companies We Keep*, 2nd ed. (White River Junction, VT: Chelsea Green, 2008).

CHAPTER 1

1. The *Whole Earth Catalog* was published from 1968 to 1971, with occasional subsequent editions.
2. For an expanded story of South Mountain Company, see John Abrams, *Companies We Keep* (White River Junction, VT: Chelsea Green, 2008).
3. John Elkington, "Enter the Triple Bottom Line," accessed April 19, 2024, https://www.johnelkington.com/archive/TBL-elkington-chapter.pdf.
4. Jim Collins, *Good to Great* (New York: Harper Business, 2001), 41.
5. Edgar Villanueva, *Decolonizing Wealth*, 2nd ed. (Oakland, CA: Berrett-Koehler, 2021), 147.
6. Andre Gide, *Travels in the Congo* (New York: Alfred Knopf, 1930), 114.
7. Max De Pree, *Leadership Is an Art* (New York: Doubleday, 1989), 9.
8. Charles Handy, *The Hungry Spirit* (New York: Broadway Books, 1999), 106–107.

CHAPTER 2

1. Brad Edmundson, *Ice Cream Social: The Struggle for the Soul of Ben and Jerry's* (San Francisco: Berrett-Koehler, 2014), 178.
2. Edmundson, 179.
3. "Make Business a Force for Good," B Lab, accessed May 1, 2024, https://www.bcorporation.net/en-us/.
4. "About B Corp Certification," B Lab, accessed May 1, 2024, https://www.bcorporation.net/en-us/certification/.
5. Ryan Honeyman and Tiffany Jana, *The B Corp Handbook* (Oakland, CA: Berrett-Koehler, 2019), 40.
6. Anjli Raval, "The Struggle for the Soul of the B Corp Movement," *Financial Times*, February 19, 2023, https://www.ft.com/content/0b632709-afda-4bdc-a6f3-bb0b02eb5a62.
7. Elizabeth Bennett, "As Greenwashing Soars, Some People Are Questioning B Corp Certification," BBC, February 6, 2024, https://www.bbc.com/worklife/article/20240202-has-b-corp-certification-turned-into-corporate-greenwashing.
8. The quote appears at LIFT Economy, home page, accessed May 2, 2024, https://www.lifteconomy.com/.
9. Yvon Chouinard, *Let My People Go Surfing* (New York: Penguin Group, 2005), 162.
10. Dean Cycon, personal conversations and correspondence, 2023.
11. Beth Spong, personal conversations and correspondence, 2023.
12. Kevin Kelly, *Excellent Advice for Living* (New York: Viking, 2023), 88.
13. Ari Weinzweig, personal conversations and correspondence, 2023.

PART TWO

1. Marjorie Kelly, *Owning Our Future* (San Francisco: Berrett-Koehler, 2012), 17.

CHAPTER 3

1. Statistics in this chapter are found across the ICA website, accessed May 1, 2024, https://ica.coop/en.
2. Oscar Perry Abello, "New York's Driver-Owned Ride-Hailing App Is Putting Its Foot on the Accelerator," *Next City*, June 13, 2023, https://nextcity.org/urbanist -news/new-yorks-driver-owned-ride-hailing-app-is-putting-its-foot-on-the -accelera.
3. "Cooperative Home Care Associates," *PHI*, accessed May 16, 2024, https://www .phinational.org/affiliate/cooperative-home-care-associates/.
4. George Cheney, Matt Noyes, Emi Do, Marcelo Vieta, Joseba Azkarraga, and Charlie Michel, *Cooperatives at Work* (Bingley, UK: Emerald Publishing, 2023), xiv.
5. ICA website.
6. John Restakis, *Humanizing the Economy* (Gabriola Island, BC: New Society Publishers, 2010), 3.
7. "Credit Union Assets, Shares, and Deposits Grow in Fourth Quarter," National Credit Union Administration, last modified March 2023, https://ncua.gov /newsroom/press-release/2023/credit-union-assets-shares-and-deposits-grow -fourth-quarter.
8. "America's Cooperative Electric Utilities," NRECA Fact Sheet, March 2024, https:// www.cooperative.com/programs-services/bts/Documents/Data/Electric-Co-op -Fact-Sheet.pdf.
9. Restakis, 237.
10. "Planning for the Future of Your Business," Northeast Transition Initiative, accessed September 20, 2004, https://ownershiptransition.org/planning-for-the-future-of -your-business/.
11. Kerala Taylor, "I Just Became a Co-Owner of My Company, and It's a Really Big Deal," *Medium*, December 14, 2021, https://keralataylor.medium.com/i-just-became -a-co-owner-of-my-company-and-its-a-really-big-deal-6a3e8bccf9f6.
12. Rob Brown, "How to Save Jobs and Build Back Better: Employee Ownership Transitions as a Key to an Equitable Economic Recovery," *Maine Policy Review* 30, no. 2 (2021): 111–115.

CHAPTER 4

1. Bruce Dobb and Tomás Durán, "Can Employee Ownership Meet Its 'Silver Tsunami' Moment?" *Nonprofit Quarterly (NPQ)*, February 21, 2024, https://nonprofitquarterly .org/can-employee-ownership-meet-its-silver-tsunami-moment/.

2. Janelle Orsi, William Lisa, and Sushil Jacob, *Legal Guide to Cooperative Conversions* (Oakland, CA: Sustainable Economies Law Center, n.d.), 7, accessed September 2, 2024, https://www.co-oplaw.org/knowledge-base/legal-guide-cooperative-conversions/.

3. Nick Romeo, *The Alternative* (New York: PublicAffairs, 2023), 184–185.

CHAPTER 5

1. "Frequently Asked Questions," Office of Advocacy, US Small Business Administration, revised December 2021, https://advocacy.sba.gov/wp-content/uploads/2021/12/Small-Business-FAQ-Revised-December-2021.pdf.

2. "Company Pay Ratios," Executive Paywatch, AFL-CIO, accessed May 8, 2024, https://aflcio.org/paywatch/company-pay-ratios.

3. Nick Romeo, *The Alternative* (New York: PublicAffairs, 2023), 10.

4. Pierre Hausemer, Angelo Di Legge, Lars Foldspang, and Peter Lange, "Summary Assessment of Emilia-Romagna," European Service Innovation Centre Report, November 2013, 1, https://ec.europa.eu/docsroom/documents/5123/attachments/1/translations/en/renditions/native.

5. John Restakis, *Humanizing the Economy* (Gabriola Island, BC: New Society Publishers, 2010), 56–57.

6. Margaret Lund and Matt Hancock, "Stewards of Enterprise: Lessons in Economic Democracy from Northern Italy," International Centre for Co-operative Management Working Paper 2020-01 (2020).

7. Lund and Hancock, 7, 9.

8. Lund and Hancock, 5.

9. Lund and Hancock, 15.

10. Lund and Hancock, 31.

11. Júlia Martins Rodrigues and Nathan Schneider, "Scaling Co-operatives through a Multi-Stakeholder Network: A Case Study in the Colorado Solar Energy Industry," *Journal of Entrepreneurial and Organizational Diversity* 10, no. 2 (2021): 40, https://doi.org/10.5947/jeod.2021.008.

12. Rodrigues and Schneider, 41–42.

13. Rodrigues and Schneider, 45.

14. Rodrigues and Schneider, 33.

15. Restakis, 257–258.

CHAPTER 6

1. Corey Rosen and John Case, *Ownership* (Oakland, CA: Berrett-Koehler, 2022), 108.

2. Rosen and Case, 85.

3. Jessica Rose, "Last Call: A Forum on the End of Employee Ownership at New Belgium," *Employee Ownership News* (blog), Fifty by Fifty, December 10, 2019, https://www.fiftybyfifty.org/2019/12/last-call-a-forum-on-the-end-of-employee-ownership-at-new-belgium/.

4. Rose.

5. Ryan Thornton, "The ESOP Holding Company: An Answer to the Failures of Private Equity," *Vermont Employee Ownership Center* (blog), August 7, 2024, https://www.veoc.org/blog/introducing-the-esop-holding-company.

CHAPTER 7

1. RSF Social Finance, "Organically Grown Company Pioneers Groundbreaking Ownership Structure to Maintain Mission & Independence in Perpetuity," July 9, 2018, https://rsfsocialfinance.org/2018/07/09/organically-grown-company-pioneers-groundbreaking-ownership-structure-to-maintain-mission-independence-in-perpetuity/.

2. Anne-Claire Broughton, Courtney Kemp, Alison Lingane, Christopher Michael, Corey Rosen, Stacey Smith, and Steve Virgil, *Using an Employee Ownership Trust for Business Transition* (San Francisco: National Center for Employee Ownership, 2024), 6–7.

3. Mark Hand, Zoe Schlag, and S. Pek, "Purposeful Succession: How Owners Can Use Purpose Trusts to Lock in Legacy and Foster Rural Community Resilience," in *Successfully Transferring Business Ownership in Small Communities*, edited by N. Walzer. Routledge (forthcoming).

4. Corey Rosen and John Case, *Ownership* (Oakland, CA: Berrett-Koehler, 2022), 181.

CHAPTER 8

1. "About Obran Cooperative," accessed August 8, 2024, https://www.obran.coop/cooperative.

2. Charity May, Jay Standish, Chelsea Robinson, Zoe Schlag, and Derek Razo, *Assets in Common* (Infrastructure for Shared Ownership, 2024), 115.

3. Rachel Phua, "Workers Funding Other Workers' Misery," *American Prospect*, October 4, 2023, https://prospect.org/labor/2023-10-04-workers-funding-misery-private-equity-pension-funds/.

4. "Our Board of Directors," Ownership Works, accessed May 31, 2024, https://ownershipworks.org/board/.

5. Jon Wertheim, "Private Equity's Unlikely Champion for Giving Workers a Leg Up with Employee Ownership," *60 Minutes*, CBS News, May 5, 2024, https://www.cbsnews.com/news/private-equitys-unlikely-champion-for-giving-workers-a-leg-up-with-employee-ownership-60-minutes-transcript/.

6. Wertheim.

7. Corey Rosen, "Private Equity and Employee Ownership" (National Center for Employee Ownership, 2024), 19.

8. Marjorie Kelly and Karen Kahn, "Is Private Equity's Employee Ownership Plan the Real Deal?" *ImpactAlpha*, July 5, 2022, https://impactalpha.com/is-private-equitys-employee-ownership-plan-the-real-deal/.

9. Nick Romeo, *The Alternative* (New York: PublicAffairs, 2023), 303.

10. Yuliya Chernova, "Backed with $245 Million, Teamshares Buys Small Businesses, Boosts Employee Ownership," *Wall Street Journal*, August 18, 2023, https://www.wsj.com/articles/backed-with-245-million-teamshares-buys-small-businesses-boosts-employee-ownership-6d6db53c.

11. Corey Rosen, 15.

CHAPTER 9

1. Bo Burlingham, *Finish Big: How Great Entrepreneurs Exit Their Companies on Top* (New York: Portfolio/Penguin, 2014), 91.

CHAPTER 10

1. Jim Collins, *Good to Great* (New York: Harper Business, 2001), 10.

2. Collins, 13.

3. Bo Burlingham, *Finish Big* (New York: Portfolio/Penguin, 2014), 91.

4. Burlingham, 115.

5. William Bridges, *Managing Transitions* (Philadelphia: Da Capo Press, 2009), 4.

6. Bridges, 141.

7. Carol Sanford, *The Regenerative Business* (Boston: Nicholas Brealey Publishing, 2017), 99.

CHAPTER 11

1. School for Democratic Management, "Democratic Management: A Practical Guide for Managers and Others," Democracy at Work Institute, 2021

2. Ari Weinzweig, *Ari's Top 5* (newsletter), July 31, 2024, https://www.zingermanscommunity.com/e-news/aris-top-5/.

3. South Mountain Company, "Operating Policies," sec. E.2(A), February 12, 2024, https://www.southmountain.com/press-and-media/category/smco-model/.

4. Alfie Kohn, *No Contest: The Case against Competition*, 2nd ed. (New York: Houghton Mifflin, 1992).

CONCLUSION

1. Carol Sanford, *The Regenerative Business* (Boston: Nicholas Brealey Publishing, 2017), 162.
2. Václav Havel, *Disturbing the Peace*, trans. Paul Wilson (New York: Knopf, 1990), 181.

RESOURCES

BOOKS AND ARTICLES

Abrams, John. *Companies We Keep*. 2nd ed. White River Junction, VT: Chelsea Green, 2008.

Bridges, William. *Managing Transitions*. Philadelphia: Da Capo Press, 2009.

Broughton, Anne-Claire, Courtney Kemp, Alison Lingane, Christopher Michael, Corey Rosen, Stacey Smith, and Steve Virgil. *Using an Employee Ownership Trust For Business Transition*. San Francisco: National Center for Employee Ownership, 2024.

Burlingham, Bo. *Finish Big: How Great Entrepreneurs Exit Their Companies on Top*. New York: Portfolio/Penguin, 2014.

Burlingham, Bo. *Small Giants: Companies That Choose to Be Great Instead of Big*. New York: Portfolio/Penguin, 2016.

Cheney, George, Matt Noyes, Emi Do, Marcelo Vieta, Joseba Azkarraga, and Charlie Michel. *Cooperatives at Work*. Bingley, UK: Emerald Publishing, 2023.

Chouinard, Yvon. *Let My People Go Surfing*. New York: Penguin Group, 2005.

Clamp, Christina, and Michael Peck. *Humanity at Work & Life: Global Diffusion of the Mondragon Cooperative Ecosystem Experience*. Cork, Ireland: Oak Tree Press, 2023.

Collins, Jim. *Good to Great*. New York: Harper Business, 2001.

De Pree, Max. *Leadership Is an Art*. New York: Doubleday, 1989.

Edmundson, Brad. *Ice Cream Social: The Struggle for the Soul of Ben and Jerry's*. San Francisco: Berrett-Koehler, 2014.

Greenleaf, Robert. *Servant Leadership*. 25th anniversary ed. Mahwah, NJ: Paulist Press, 2002.

Greider, William. *Come Home, America*. New York: Rodale, 2009.

Honeyman, Ryan, and Tiffany Jana. *The B Corp Handbook*. Oakland, CA: Berrett-Koehler, 2019.

Kelly, Marjorie. *Owning Our Future*. San Francisco: Berrett-Koehler, 2012.

Kelly, Marjorie. *Wealth Supremacy*. Oakland, CA: Berrett-Koehler, 2023.

Kohn, Alfie. *No Contest: The Case against Competition.* 2nd ed. New York: Houghton Mifflin, 1992.

Logue, John, and Jacquelyn Yates. *The Real World of Employee Ownership.* Ithaca, NY: ILR Press/Cornell University Press, 2001.

Lund, Margaret, and Matt Hancock. "Stewards of Enterprise: Lessons in Economic Democracy from Northern Italy." International Centre for Co-operative Management Working Paper 2020-01 (2020). https://www.smu.ca/webfiles/WorkingPaper2020-01.pdf.

May, Charity, Jay Standish, Chelsea Robinson, Zoe Schlag, and Derek Razo. *Assets in Common: Stories of Business and Community Leaders Remaking the Economy from the Ground Up.* San Francisco: Infrastructure for Shared Ownership, 2024.

Meadows, Donella. *Thinking in Systems.* White River Junction, VT: Chelsea Green, 2008.

Morrison, Roy. *We Build the Road As We Travel.* London, UK, Blond and Briggs, 1973.

Orsi, Janelle, William Lisa, and Sushil Jacob. *Legal Guide to Cooperative Conversions.* Oakland, CA: Sustainable Economies Law Center, n.d. Accessed September 2, 2024. https://www.co-oplaw.org/knowledge-base/legal-guide-cooperative-conversions/.

Parks, Sharon Daloz. *Leadership Can Be Taught.* Boston: Harvard Business School Press, 2005.

Restakis, John. *Humanizing the Economy.* Gabriola Island, BC: New Society Publishers, 2010.

Romeo, Nick. *The Alternative: How to Build a Just Economy.* New York: PublicAffairs, 2023.

Rosen, Corey, and John Case. *Ownership.* Oakland, CA: Berrett-Koehler, 2022.

Rosen, Corey, John Case, and Martin Staubus. *Equity.* Brighton, MA: Harvard Business Review Press, 2005.

Sanford, Carol. *The Regenerative Business.* Boston, MA: Nicholas Brealey Publishing, 2017.

Schneider, Nathan. *Everything for Everyone.* New York: Nation Books, 2018.

School for Democratic Management. "Democratic Management: A Practical Guide for Managers and Others." Democracy at Work Institute, 2021. https://democracy.institute.coop/democratic-management-practical-guide-managers-and-others.

Schumacher, E. F. *Small Is Beautiful.* New York: Harper Perennial, 2010. Originally published by Blond & Briggs, London, 1973.

Smith, Stacey, and Steve Virgil. *Using an Employee Ownership Trust for Business Transition.* San Francisco: National Center for Employee Ownership, 2024.

Speth, James Gustave. *America the Possible.* New Haven, CT: Yale University Press, 2012.

Stack, Jack, and Bo Burlingham. *The Great Game of Business.* New York: Crown Currency, 2013.

Villanueva, Edgar. *Decolonizing Wealth.* 2nd ed. Oakland, CA: Berrett-Koehler, 2021.

Weinzweig, Ari. *Zingerman's Guide to Good Leading, Part 1: A Lapsed Anarchist's Approach to Building a Great Business.* Ann Arbor, MI: Zingerman's Press, 2010.

Weinzweig, Ari. *Zingerman's Guide to Good Leading, Part 2: A Lapsed Anarchist's Approach to Being a Better Leader.* Ann Arbor, MI: Zingerman's Press, 2012.

Weinzweig, Ari. *Zingerman's Guide to Good Leading, Part 3: A Lapsed Anarchist's Approach to Managing Ourselves.* Ann Arbor, MI: Zingerman's Press, 2013.

Weinzweig, Ari. *Zingerman's Guide to Good Leading, Part 4: A Lapsed Anarchist's Approach to the Power of Beliefs in Business.* Ann Arbor, MI: Zingerman's Press, 2016.

VALUABLE INFORMATION

The websites of the following organizations provide extensive employee ownership resources, information, and research:

Certified EO
    www.certifiedeo.com
Common Trust
    common-trust.com
The Democracy Collaborative
    www.democracycollaborative.org
Democracy at Work Institute
    institute.coop
Employee Ownership Expansion Network
    eoxnetwork.org
EO+WD
    eowd.org
The ESOP Association
    esopassociation.org
Fifty by Fifty
    fiftybyfifty.org
ICA Group
    icagroup.org
National Center for Employee Ownership
    nceo.org
Northeast Transition Initiative
    ownershiptransition.org
Project Equity
    project-equity.org
Sustainable Economies Law Center
    theselc.org
    co-oplaw.org

University of Wisconsin Center for Cooperatives
uwcc.wisc.edu
U.S. Federation of Worker Cooperatives
www.usworker.coop

EMPLOYEE OWNERSHIP DEVELOPMENT CONSULTANTS

Abrams+Angell
abramsangell.com
Worker cooperatives
Cooperative Development Institute/Business Ownership Solutions
cdi.coop/business-ownership-solutions
Worker cooperatives
EOT Law
eotlaw.com/people
Employee ownership trusts
The ESOP Association
esopassociation.org
ESOPs
ICA Group
ica-group.org
Employee ownership, all types
Jason Wiener | p.c.
jrwiener.com
Employee ownership, all types
Praxis Consulting
praxiscg.com
Employee ownership, all types
The National Center of Employee Ownership
nceo.org
Employee ownership, all types
Project Equity
project-equity.org
Worker cooperatives and Employee ownership trusts
Purpose Owned
purposeowned.com
Employee ownership trusts
University of Wisconsin Center for Cooperatives
uwcc.wisc.edu
Worker co-ops

Vermont Employee Ownership Center
veoc.org
Employee ownership, all types

This next resource has an extensive list of additional consulting companies and organizations:

Workers to Owners Collaborative
becomingemployeeowned.org/workers-to-owners

SOURCES OF CAPITAL AND FINANCING

Capital Impact Partners
capitalimpact.org
Concerned Capital
concernedcapital.org
Cooperative Fund of the Northeast
cooperativefund.org
Kachuwa Fund
kachuwaimpactfund.org
Local Enterprise Assistance Fund (LEAF)
leaffund.org
National Cooperative Bank
ncb.coop
Seed Commons
seedcommons.org
Shared Capital Cooperative
sharedcapital.coop
The Working World
theworkingworld.org

ACKNOWLEDGMENTS

When I open a book, I often read the acknowledgments first. They are, after all, the story of the book. And the acknowledgments that follow are, indeed, the story of this one, which really began in 1994.

That's when I became a writer, of sorts. Kevin Ireton, then editor of *Fine Homebuilding* magazine, asked me to write an essay for an annual feature called "Taking Issue." Having never written for a national publication, I worked, reworked, massaged, and adjusted my writing until I thought I nailed it. I faxed it to Kevin (in those pre-internet days), and in a few hours it came back. I took one look, and my heart sank. The cross-outs and scrawled notes nearly obscured the typed essay that I had labored over for weeks. I called Kevin.

He said, "Hey, John, want to talk?"

I gulped and said yes.

He asked me about the first line of the essay, "What did you mean to say?"

I told him, and he said, "Good. Then say that."

We continued down the page, processing his comments, until I had an epiphany. I suddenly understood what an editor does, and that it is an extraordinarily generous line of work, the hidden hand behind the writing, helping us express ourselves better than we otherwise could. Ever since that moment, I have honored and enjoyed the process of having my writing read and edited by others. Kevin has become a close friend.

Kim, Jamie, Steve, and Clark

There are four people without whom this book would not exist.

As I approached my South Mountain retirement in 2022 and considered writing this book, I thought I might be fooling myself. I wasn't certain I could muster the energy to write it the way I wanted to. My partner Kim Angell thought I was selling myself short. Her faith helped to propel me forward. She has provided constant support. Thanks for being with me, Kim.

For decades, I have been engaged in discussion and endeavors regarding business and community with my friend Jamie Wolf. Until his recent retirement, Jamie ran a design/build remodeling company that converted to a worker cooperative before his departure. Our ongoing conversations always challenge me to think harder. And better.

Once I developed a book proposal, I set out to engage a publisher that embodies the book's values. I had a list of one—Berrett-Koehler (BK). My friend Marjorie Kelly (who has published three books with BK) agreed to introduce me to Steve Piersanti, the founder, former CEO, and now senior editor. But she said to be careful what I wished for, because Steve's a taskmaster who would challenge me relentlessly.

I sent Steve the proposal, we talked, and he told me that he liked the idea, but the proposal needed work. A ton of it. He helped me revise it to make it suitable for the BK editorial and publications committees. Marjorie, who is a fearless thinker, brilliant writer, and good friend who has inspired me for decades, helped me with the proposal too.

Steve and I have had countless cross-country video meetings, but, to this day, we have never met in person. I'm sure we will soon. Taskmaster? Well, maybe. But our work together has been a journey of pure joy. I've loved every minute and every aspect of our collaboration. I've become one of the many people in the world of books who deeply admire Steve.

Clark Hanjian is a Buddhist chaplain, mediator, and top-notch editor. He worked with me from the start—editing, formatting, and cleaning up my mess. Clark has an extraordinary range of skills and focuses with clarity and rigor. He is the perfect complement to my feel-your-way, sometimes-distracted approach. He is blunt but always kind and has helped with this project in more ways than I can count.

I cannot adequately express my gratitude to these people who have been essential to this project.

The Readers

When I completed the draft manuscript, seven people reviewed it. Three of them were hired by Berrett-Koehler (a practice BK does with each book it publishes). They were Christopher Arnold, John Case, and Gabriel Grant. Well chosen, to say the least.

The other four were people I asked to read it, who generously agreed: Carolyn Edsell-Vetter of the Cooperative Fund of the Northeast; Deirdre Bohan, who replaced me as South Mountain CEO; and Jamie Wolf and Kevin Ireton, close friends mentioned above.

These seven amazing readers provided diverse opinions and suggested many valuable edits. I was faced with a mountain of material to understand and assemble into a rewrite. It was like a 1,000-piece jigsaw puzzle. They made this book a much better one.

Alex Moss of Praxis Consulting Group read parts of the book and helped me shape it along the way. He is one of the most knowledgeable and thoughtful employee ownership people I know.

And then there's Ari Weinzweig. I'm grateful to him for his friendship and deeply honored that he agreed to write the Foreword. As if he doesn't have enough to do.

The Interviews

To write chapters 3 through 8 on employee ownership, I realized I didn't know enough about the subject, even though I've lived it and thought about it for nearly forty years. So I made a list of knowledgeable people in the field and leaders of companies and asked each if they would spend an hour talking with me. Many of the interviews led to other recommendations and introductions. I ended up doing more than sixty interviews, recording them, doing AI transcriptions, poring over pages of text that resulted from each, and often following up with more questions. There are two great things about this interview method: (1) you have an accurate recording of the conversation and (2) because the recording is being transcribed, you don't have to take notes or remember anything. You can be entirely present in the conversation, and that makes for better conversations.

I am deeply grateful to these storytellers and resource people: Aaron Dawson, Alex Moss, Allison Curtis, Andy Danforth, Beck Sydow, Beth Spong, Blake Jones, Bo Burlingham, Bob Gelser, Brad Edmundson, Brad Hermann, Brett Tolley, Cameron Madill, Carolyn Edsell-Vetter, Chip Cargas, Chris Michael, C. J. Young, Corey Rosen, Courtney Berner, Dan Fireside, Danny Spitzberg, David Hammer, David Korten, Dean Cycon, Debby Straight, Declan Keefe, Derek Razo, Erbin Crowell, Eric Rieger, Fortunat Mueller, Frank Cetera, Graeme Nuttall, Greg Brodsky, Hendrix Berry, Hilary Abell, Jason Wiener, Jay Coen-Gilbert, Jay Ward, Jen Briggs, Jennie Msall, Jenny Everett, Jessica Mason, Joel Williamson, John McMicken, Jonathan Orpin, Kevin Kennedy, Larry Filipsky, Loren Rodgers, Margaret Lund, Mark Hand, Matthias Scheiblehner, Meegan Moriarty, Melissa Hoover, Michael Brownrigg, Miriam Gee, Molly Hemstreet, Natalie Reitman-White, Rich Hussey, Rick Dubrow, Rob Brown, Ryan Honeyman, Sara Chester, Sarah Kautz, Sebastian Kimura, Shawn Berry, Stephen Irvin, Steve Storkan, Zarin Kresge.

Some of these people are friends. Some of them became friends. Some offered stories or intelligence that didn't make it through the book's final edit but would have if there were more space.

Berrett-Koehler and Weaving Influence

The BK community has been supportive and helpful in every way. I'm deeply impressed with the devotion of BK authors and board members to the company. And the staff, to a person, has been a tremendous pleasure to work with. Besides Steve, my primary interactions as of this writing have been with Jeevan Sivasubramaniam, Praveen Madan, Christy Kirk, and Ashley Ingram (and there have been others). I particularly appreciate the cover design work by Ashley, and I am grateful for the skilful copyreading and book design of Grace Weir, Michelle Witkowski, and their colleagues at Westchester Publishing.

Early on, Steve told me that BK would help to market my book and spread its message, but that I would have to do significantly more. He recommended that I hire a book marketing firm. After I spoke with Becky Robinson, the founder of Weaving Influence, a fruitful collaboration began that continues to this day. Thanks so much to Becky and all at Weaving Influence, including Allyson Jansen, Aubrey Pastorek, and Elizabeth Mars.

John Magnifico is a graphic designer in Massachusetts who South Mountain has worked with for years. He helped to craft the first draft for this book's cover, my presentation for BK's Author Day, website alterations, and other stellar graphic work.

Others Who Influenced Me along the Way

Then there are the people who have influenced me during the life journey that brought me here. My children, Pinto and Sophie, their spouses, and their children (my six grandsons) come first. I love them all deeply and dearly. Their mother, Chris Hudson Abrams, was my wife and fellow traveler for forty-seven years, until she died in 2017 after a prolonged battle with cancer.

My parents, Marilyn and Herb Abrams, who died in 2016 and 2017, at ages 93 and 95, respectively, supported me in so many ways that can't be counted or measured or even fully recalled. They were always there for me, even when our paths diverged in difficult ways. The same goes for my sister Nancy.

Merle Adams, who died way too young, at age 62, taught me about the beauty of tolerance and overcoming differences. We disagreed about almost everything—religion and politics in particular—except the things that actually matter. Our friendship was filled with love and laughter.

My friend Jonathan Orpin has taught me about the power of conviction and that there's no such thing as giving up.

Other friends and family members, far too many to list, have influenced the way I think and learn and live.

And then there are all the people I've worked with in the world of affordable housing over the last forty years and my many friends at the Northeast Sustainable Energy Association, Building Energy Bottom Lines, and a host of other organizations—thank you for the comradery, inspiration, and shared vision.

The heroes of this story, to whom I'm deeply indebted, are my friends, colleagues, and co-owners at South Mountain Company and our many trade partners and advisers over the last fifty years—people from both the past and present. These are the people with whom I spent my working life in the trenches, in loving and sometimes tough collaboration.

But none of that work would have happened without our hundreds of amazing clients, some of whom have become close lifelong friends. Some are families with whom we are now working with the second and third generation. I treasure them all.

Heroes, too, are the people who work in in the companies that I profile in this book, most of whom I don't even know.

I've already expressed gratitude to many here, but gratitude is something worth expressing more than once. So to each of you, I again say thank you.

INDEX

ABOUT THE AUTHOR

I always read and I always wrote. From kindergarten through seventh grade, I was a star student. Then I turned rebellious and discarded academic aspirations. But I did fancy myself a writer, and editing the school newspaper was about the only productive thing I did in high school. Growing up in the Bay Area, I spent more time hanging out at Kepler's Bookstore in Menlo Park than doing schoolwork.

After hitchhiking from Berkeley to Connecticut in 1967, I briefly attended Wesleyan University (becoming the first person in the class of 1971 to drop out) and then Marlboro College in Vermont, where I met my wife-to-be, Chris Hudson. The classroom just wasn't for me. A different world beckoned. Chris and I (and our son Pinto, born in 1970) embraced the back-to-the-land movement, traveling from Vermont to Northern California to Oregon to British Columbia and back to Vermont over a five-year period. The *Whole Earth Catalog* became my curriculum and guidebook, opening doors to realms I'd never imagined. We helped to build communes, bought old farms, fixed beat-up houses, learned arcane agrarian and backwoods skills, and practiced homespun Buddhism with a dose of political activism thrown in for balance.

I became passionate about craft and wood and building and design. After making a few handmade houses in Vermont and opening a woodworking shop in 1973, an opportunity to build a house on Martha's Vineyard presented itself. We moved there and never left.

South Mountain Company, the inadvertent seat-of-the-pants company I co-founded, became a sole proprietorship when my partner Mitchell Posin departed in 1986. With my colleagues, I converted it into a worker cooperative. My love for buildings mixed well with my devotion to collaborative enterprise, and South Mountain became an emblematic integrated architecture, building, and solar company. Our community activism included leading the local effort to offset high-end second homes with top quality zero-energy affordable housing—and doing the requisite policy work and fundraising.

As I managed the business, I engaged in a variety of public activities in the arenas of socially responsible business and high-performance building, and I continued to write. During a 2004–2005 sabbatical, I wrote *The Company We Keep;* the second edition, *Companies We Keep* (2008), is still in print today. Since 2009, I have maintained a blog called *Companies We Keep.* After retiring from South Mountain in 2022 and passing the reins to next-generation leadership, I formed Abrams+Angell with my late-in-life partner Kim Angell to guide worker cooperative conversions and help small businesses achieve social, environmental, and financial goals.

My affordable housing work continues as I serve on the executive committee of the Coalition to Create the Martha's Vineyard Housing Bank, as does the work I have been doing with the Northeast Sustainable Energy Association (for the past forty years) and Building Energy Bottom Lines (for the past ten years).

Martha's Vineyard has been home for fifty years. My two children and six grandsons (and Kim's three kids, too) were raised here. After my wife Chris died in 2017, I was deeply fortunate to find Kim. My life experiences have left me, at age 75, with a robust sense that audacious hope and cautious optimism—mixed with love and kindness—are the most powerful tools we have for change.

Berrett–Koehler
Publishers

Berrett-Koehler is an independent publisher dedicated to an ambitious mission: *Connecting people and ideas to create a world that works for all.*

Our publications span many formats, including print, digital, audio, and video. We also offer online resources, training, and gatherings. And we will continue expanding our products and services to advance our mission.

We believe that the solutions to the world's problems will come from all of us, working at all levels: in our society, in our organizations, and in our own lives. Our publications and resources offer pathways to creating a more just, equitable, and sustainable society. They help people make their organizations more humane, democratic, diverse, and effective (and we don't think there's any contradiction there). And they guide people in creating positive change in their own lives and aligning their personal practices with their aspirations for a better world.

And we strive to practice what we preach through what we call "The BK Way." At the core of this approach is *stewardship,* a deep sense of responsibility to administer the company for the benefit of all of our stakeholder groups, including authors, customers, employees, investors, service providers, sales partners, and the communities and environment around us. Everything we do is built around stewardship and our other core values of *quality, partnership, inclusion,* and *sustainability.*

We are grateful to our readers, authors, and other friends who are supporting our mission. We ask you to share with us examples of how BK publications and resources are making a difference in your lives, organizations, and communities at bkconnection.com/impact.

Dear reader,

Thank you for picking up this book and welcome to the worldwide BK community! You're joining a special group of people who have come together to create positive change in their lives, organizations, and communities.

What's BK all about?

Our mission is to connect people and ideas to create a world that works for all.

Why? Our communities, organizations, and lives get bogged down by old paradigms of self-interest, exclusion, hierarchy, and privilege. But we believe that can change. That's why we seek the leading experts on these challenges—and share their actionable ideas with you.

A welcome gift

To help you get started, we'd like to offer you a **free copy** of one of our bestselling ebooks:

bkconnection.com/welcome

When you claim your **free ebook**, you'll also be subscribed to our blog.

Our freshest insights

Access the best new tools and ideas for leaders at all levels on our blog at ideas.bkconnection.com.

Sincerely,

Your friends at Berrett-Koehler

MIX
Paper | Supporting responsible forestry
FSC® C005010